Stikky® Stock Charts

Stikky® Stock Charts

LEARN THE 8 MAJOR STOCK CHART PATTERNS USED BY PROFESSIONALS
AND HOW TO INTERPRET THEM TO TRADE SMART—IN ONE HOUR, GUARANTEED.

LAURENCE HOLT BOOKS
New York

© 2004-7 Laurence Holt Books, Inc
www.stikky.com

303 Park Avenue South, #1030
New York, NY 10010

First printing October 2003

Library of Congress Cataloging-in-Publication Data on file.

Cover design and illustrations by Cate Shannon.
Charts created at www.prophet.net.

ISBN 1-932974-00-8

10 9 8 7

Printed in Canada

What this book is about

Stikky Stock Charts uses a powerful learning method to teach anyone the signals that professional traders use to make buy and sell decisions, step-by-step.

Each step builds on what came before and reinforces it. That way, by the time you reach the end of the book, you will be confident in reading a stock chart and forecasting the most likely next move.

Still more exciting, the things you learn will serve as 'hooks' on which you can hang future knowledge about stock chart trends and patterns.

The book also explains how to set a *stop loss*, which can help you to minimize your trading losses and maximize your gains.

Stikky Stock Charts has four parts:

- **Sequence One** tells you how to identify trends and draw *trendlines*, *support lines*, and *resistance lines*. It also teaches you to recognize *channels* and *rectangles,* how to use them to make investment decisions, and how to place an order with a broker. *If possible, you should read this sequence in one sitting.*

- **Sequence Two** builds on what you learned in Sequence One, adding several patterns: the *megaphone*, three types of *triangle*, the *double top,* and the *head and shoulders top.* It also tells you how to read *volume*, what a *stop loss* is, and how to set one. *Ideally, you should leave a few days, but no more than a week, between completing Sequence One and reading Sequence Two.*

- **The Epilogue**, a special feature of Stikky books, brings together everything you have learned and reinforces it in some new and unfamiliar situations. *Again, you should leave a few days between completing Sequence Two and reading the Epilogue.*

- If, by the end of the book, you are hungry to find out more, as we hope you will be, you will find dozens of things to explore in the **Next Steps** section.

You can skip to the Next Steps section at any time, of course, but the rest of the book only makes sense if read in order: Sequence One, Sequence Two, Epilogue.

How to read this book

Learning with *Stikky Stock Charts* may be different from how you are used to learning. Please read this page carefully.

First, read Sequence One which runs from the next page to the **Pause point** on page 121. That should take only 30 minutes (but don't worry if it takes longer).

We find people get more out of the book if they stop there and practice what they have learned for real. We'd like you to do the same.

Then, after a few days, read Sequence Two. If you are away from the book for more than a week, you may find it helpful to review some of Sequence One before starting Sequence Two.

Many people think the stock market is too complex for them to understand. Some have a 'mental block' about it. If that describes you, remember this: everything in this book is simply about finding patterns on a piece of paper.

To get the most from *Stikky Stock Charts*:

- Relax and take your time

- Don't worry about taking notes

- Don't worry about memorizing anything

- Try to avoid being interrupted

- Don't just visualize lines, draw them on the chart.

Most importantly, by turning this page you promise yourself that, when asked a question in the text, you will not flip ahead until you have tried to answer it.

(Flipping backwards to review pages you have already covered is fine.)

Keep this promise and what you learn will stick.

Sequence One

A distant relative has left you $100,000 in Acme Corp stock plus $100,000 in cash.

Here is the recent stock chart for Acme.

You have to decide whether to sell the stock. Or do you use the cash to buy more stock? Or do you wait and see?

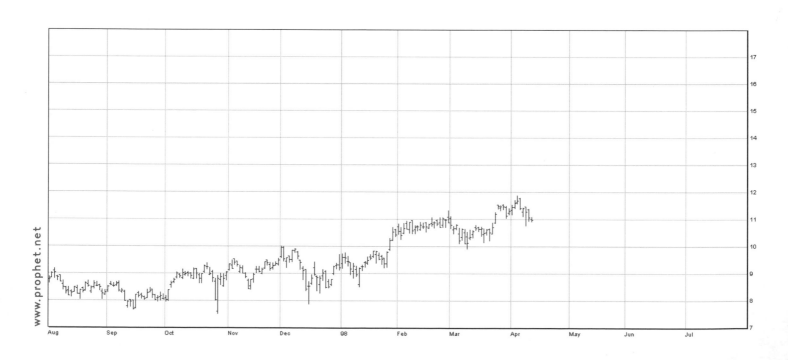

www.prophet.net

Aug   Sep   Oct   Nov   Dec   98   Feb   Mar   Apr   May   Jun   Jul

Most people would say they
needed more information about
Acme Corp: its business, its
management, its prospects, etc.

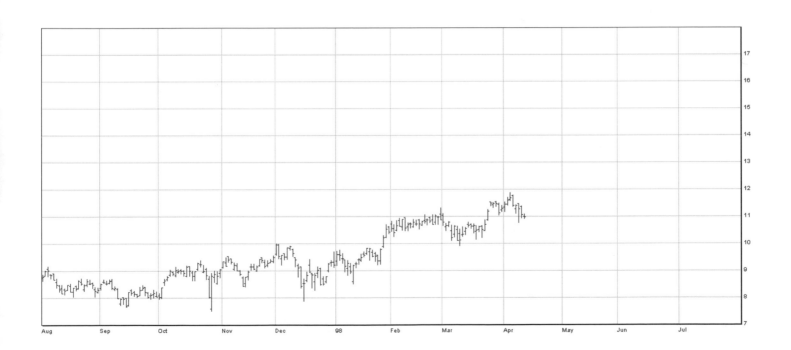

But consider this: stock market professionals, who follow the market every day, already know all that information.

And they have already acted on it.

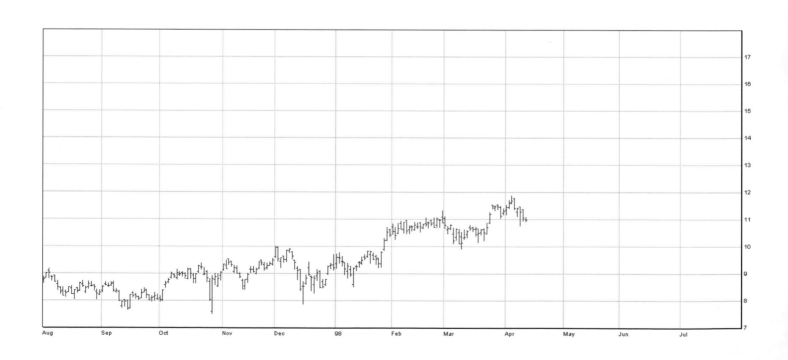

If they believed Acme was
under valued, they would have
bought it, and the price would
now be higher.

If they believed Acme was
over valued, they would have
sold it, and the price would
now be lower.

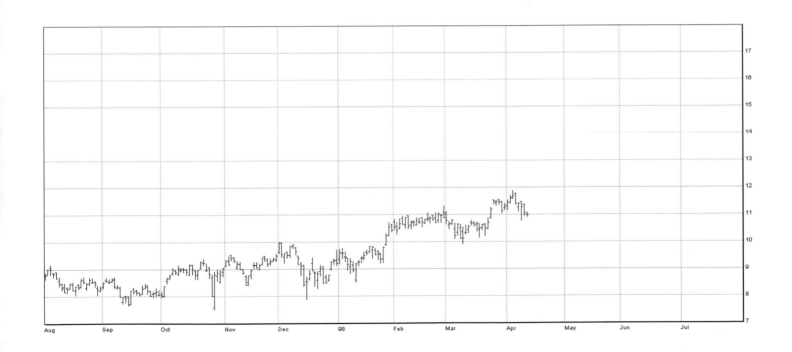

In other words, all of that information about Acme Corp is *already in the chart*.

Of course, you could go and read the information anyway. But would you wind up with any better insight than the market in general?

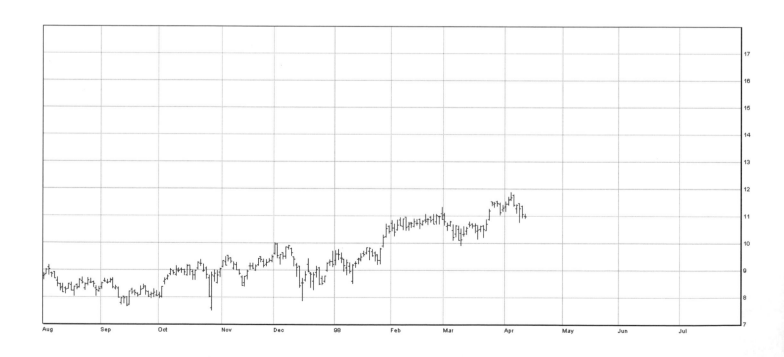

There is an easier way.

According to 'technical analysts', all you need is to read the chart.

And recent research has backed up that claim—information in the chart can sometimes be used to predict future prices.

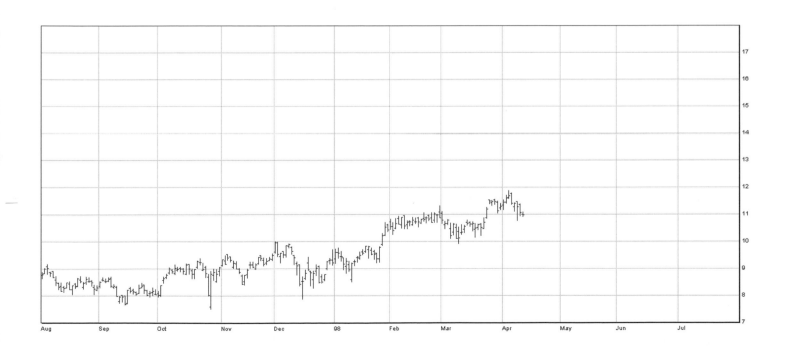

In fact, professional traders make many of their decisions using a few simple patterns that occur again and again in the charts.

This book will teach you to find those patterns. At the end of it, reading charts like Acme's will be second nature.

But first, some basics…

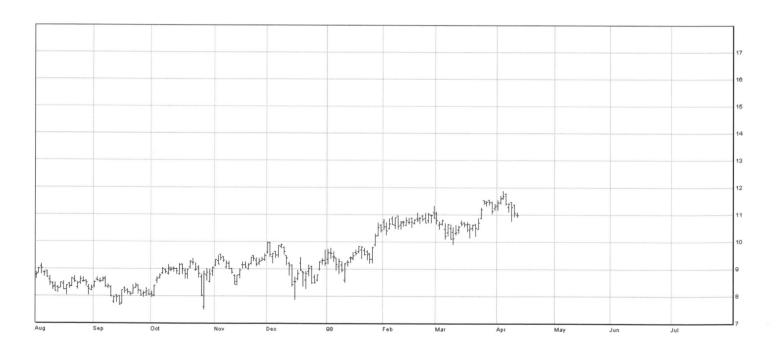

Here's another typical stock
chart (we'll come back to
Acme). Let's zoom in on the last
part of it…

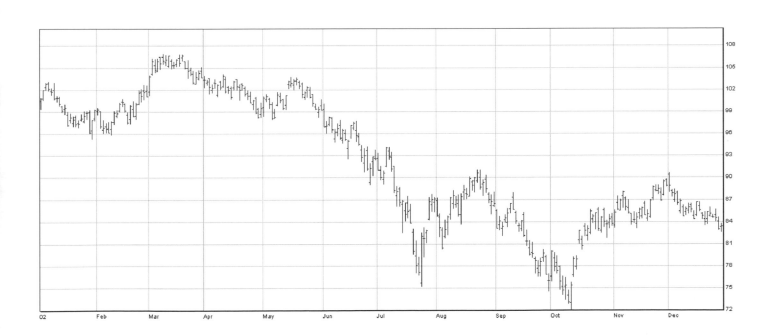

It's made up of vertical bars.

Zooming in even further…

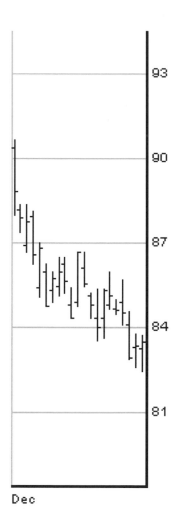

...you can see that each bar tells you a lot.

The top and bottom of the bar tell you the highest and lowest prices that the stock reached that day.

This stock reached a high of $84.60 and a low of $82.90.

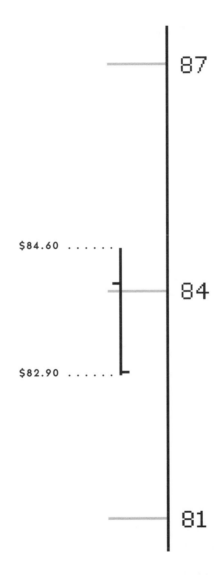

The stubs on the left and right side of the bar tell you what the price was at the start and end of the day.

But it turns out that they are not usually much help in finding trends and patterns, so don't worry about the stubs.

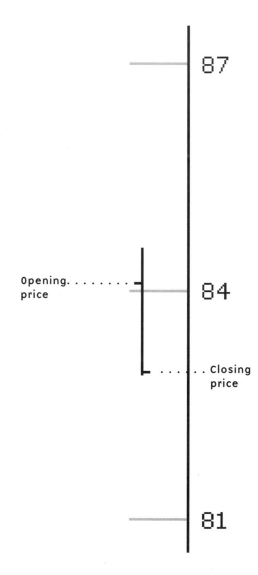

87

Opening.
price

84

Closing
price

81

Zooming back out, you can see
how the stock price moved over
a series of days, in this case
December 2002.

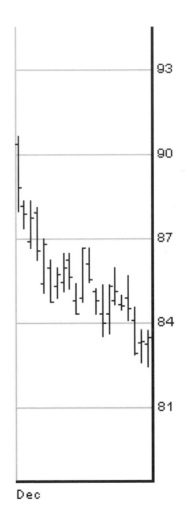

(If the market is closed—on a weekend, say, or a holiday such as Christmas Day—there are no bars for that day. As far as the stock chart is concerned, those days simply don't exist.)

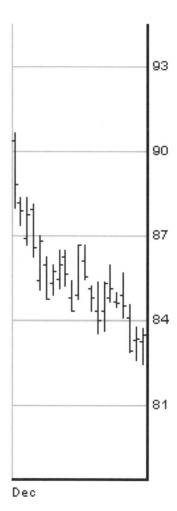

Dec

Okay, so what is the lowest price for this stock across the whole period?

Go ahead and figure it out before flipping the page.

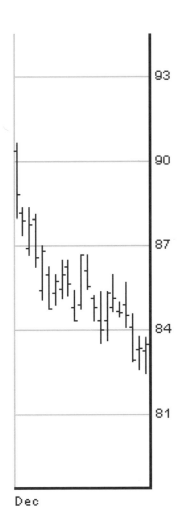

Halfway between $81 and $84: $82.50.

And what's the highest price for this period?

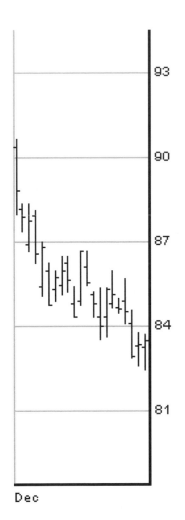

Dec

A little way above $90
($90.60 in fact).

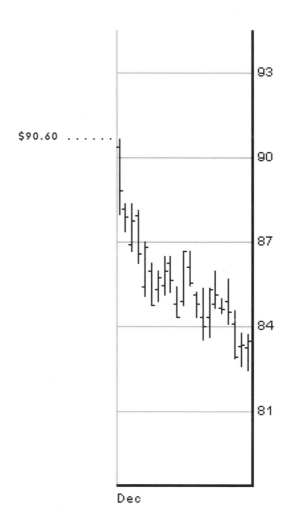

Notice that the bottom of the bars on this chart seem to lie along a line. This line is important—it's called a 'trendline'.

When professionals see a stock chart, the first thing they do is draw lines like this wherever three or more bars line up.

You are about to do the same. So take a good look at where this line is drawn.

Trendlines must touch at least
three separate bars.

This one touches four.

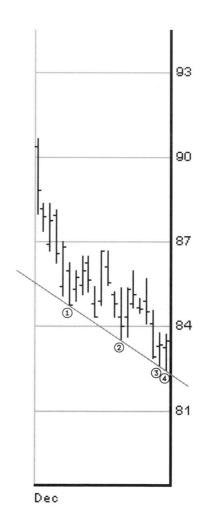

Okay, your turn.

Take a ruler and a pencil and draw a trendline across the bottom of the bars on this chart.

(To learn chart patterns properly, you really need to draw the line, not just visualize it.)

Flip back to compare your trendline with this one. Does it connect the same bars?

A trendline connecting the low points of a chart, like this one does, is called a lower trendline.

Being able to draw trendlines is a key skill. When mastered, it will allow you to forecast future price movements. So it's worth a little more practice.

Draw a lower trendline for
this chart.

(Bear in mind that trendlines
can slope upwards as well as
downwards.)

Did you draw one of these three lines? They are valid trendlines, but there is a better one.

Better trendlines touch more bars and touch bars spread over a greater distance, which shows that the trend is persistent.

Or did you draw this? It's also a valid trendline—it slightly crosses a bar, which is okay as long as it's only one or two bars.

But we are looking for the most recent trend (the one furthest to the right)…

…which is this one.

So, try drawing a lower trendline on this chart.

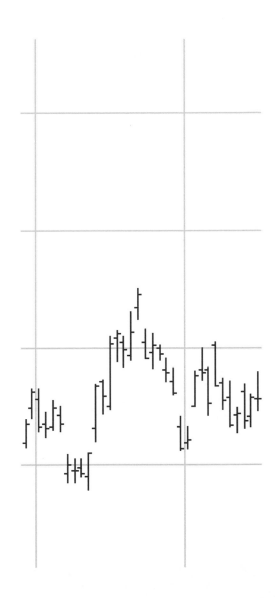

Here is the line we drew.

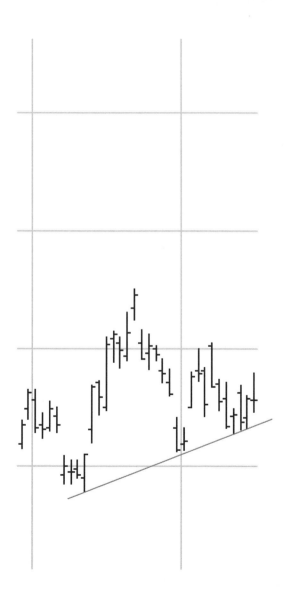

It's not a perfect fit—points ② and ③ don't quite touch the trendline—but there are another four that are a good fit.

The fit is almost never perfect, but the better it is, the better the trendline.

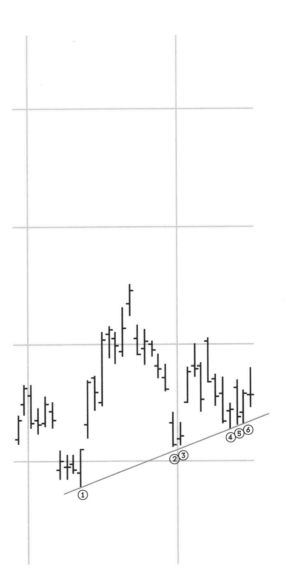

If you connected the tops of bars rather than the bottoms, you drew an upper trendline not a lower trendline.

(We'll cover upper trendlines in a moment. You're ahead of the game.)

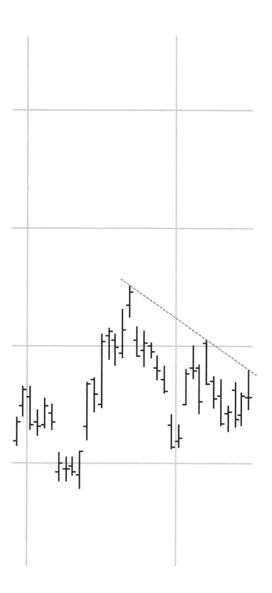

Often, you will be able to find more than one trendline to draw.

Those that connect the most recent bars (at the right of the chart) are called short-term trendlines.

They are useful for very active traders who buy or sell every few days or hours.

Short-term trendline

Feb   Mar   Apr

Trendlines that connect more distant bars across a larger area of the chart are called medium-term trendlines—useful for people who buy or sell every few weeks or months.

We assume you are going to hold on to an investment longer than a day, so you can completely ignore short-term trendlines from here on.

Medium-term trendline

Short-term trendline

Feb   Mar   Apr

The medium-term trendlines you are looking for extend across at least a month and probably several months.

So find the medium-term trendline in this chart.

If your trendline was shorter than this, you may want to go back and re-read the last few pages.

(You may notice that one of the bars protrudes a little way through the trendline—that's allowed here because there are several other good touches.)

Feb   Mar

Now draw the medium-term *upper* trendline on this chart (so connect the very tops of bars, not the bottoms).

Apr   May   Jun

This is more like a real
stock chart.

Draw a lower trendline here
(so connect the bottoms of bars).

Remember, you're looking for
a trendline that covers more
than one month, possibly
several months.

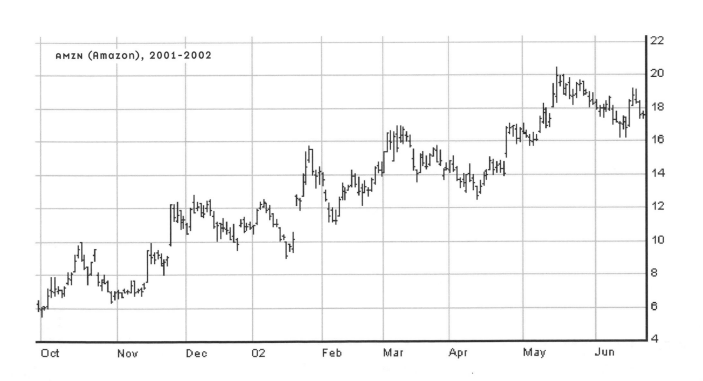

AMZN (Amazon), 2001-2002

This line has three good touches
and some other near touches.
It cuts the chart in mid-January
but that's allowed since it's only
one bar.

AMZN (Amazon), 2001-2002

Maybe you drew this line. It is
valid too, though it lasts only
just over a month.

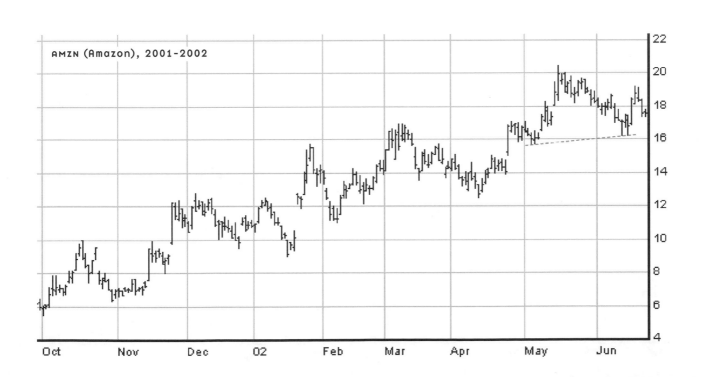

AMZN (Amazon), 2001-2002

Or perhaps you drew one of these two? Each of these lines only has two good touches.

(Where we show charts for real stocks, we put the name of the stock at the top—this is Amazon's stock price for 2001-2002.)

AMZN (Amazon), 2001-2002

There are two lower trendlines to find on this chart for Dell Computer.

One covers most of the width of the chart—find it first.

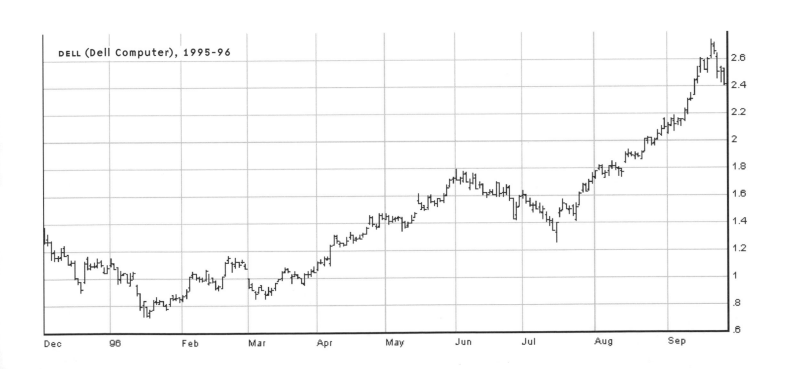

DELL (Dell Computer), 1995-96

Don't worry if you don't get the
exact same position as this—even
the experts sometimes disagree.

DELL (Dell Computer), 1995-96

Now find the other lower trendline, which covers a couple of months.

If you find more than one, we want the most recent (rightmost) since that tells us what the chart might do next.

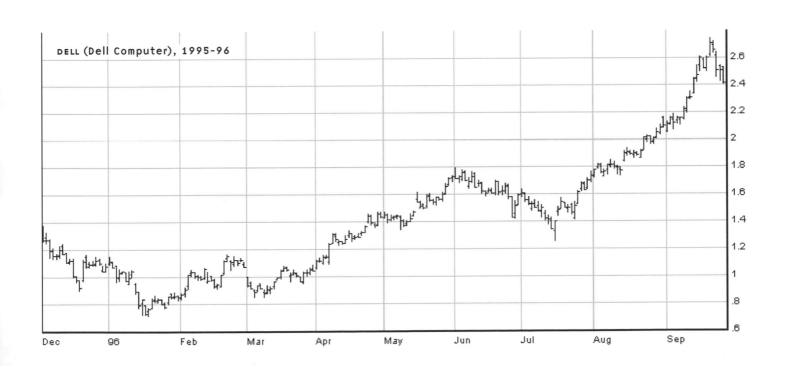

DELL (Dell Computer), 1995–96

The solid line shows the
trendline we were looking for.
The dotted line is a weaker
trendline (fewer touches) and is
too old to be useful.

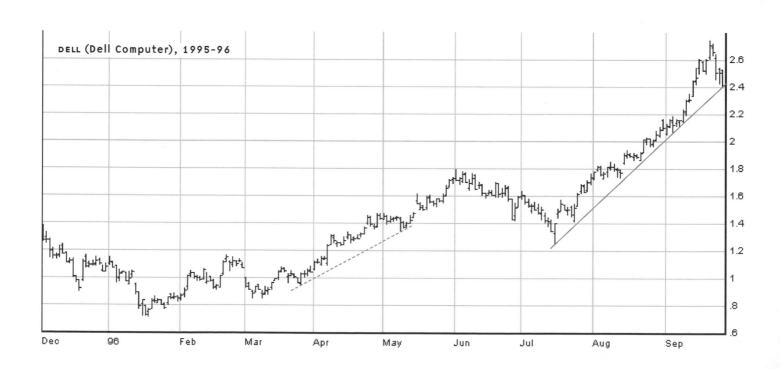

DELL (Dell Computer), 1995-96

Now draw an upper trendline and a lower trendline on this piece of a chart.

Don't flip the page until you find both trendlines (unless you really have to).

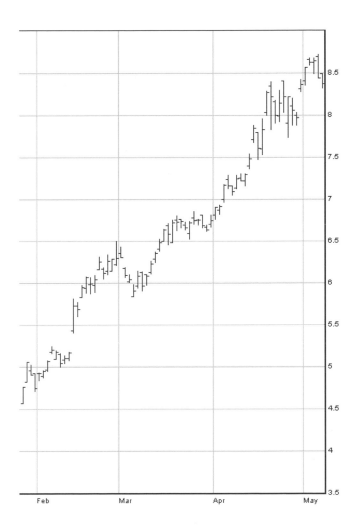

Again, don't worry whether you got the exact same lines—just as long as your lines have three or more touches and spread across more than one month.

Upper and lower trendlines aren't always parallel, but when they are it's called a 'channel'.

This is the chart for Motorola for late 1999 and all of 2000.

Your job is to draw as many valid *upper* medium-term trendlines (ie, across more than one month) as you can find.

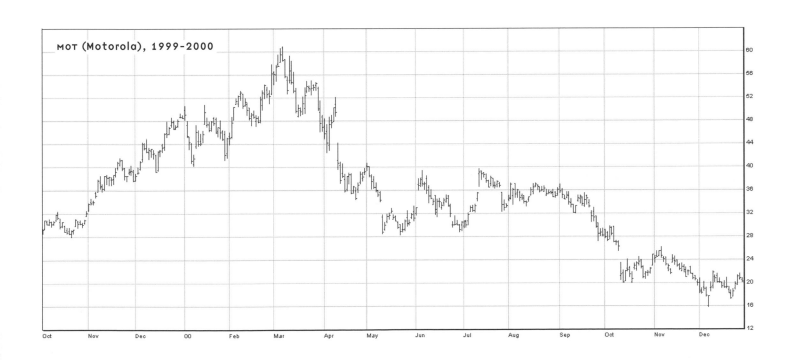

MOT (Motorola), 1999-2000

There are at least 9.

If you found different lines, check that they are valid (ie, have three touches or more) and medium-term (more than a month long).

MOT (Motorola), 1999-2000

You may think 9 is a lot for a year…but look how many lower trendlines there are in the same chart: 15.

Which means that you should have no problem finding a trendline for almost any stock chart.

MOT (Motorola), 1999-2000

One of these lines is unusual: it's horizontal. We'll see why these lines are particularly helpful later in this Sequence.

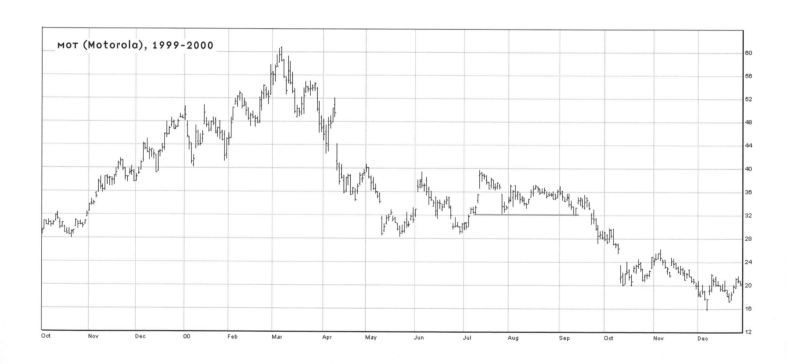

MOT (Motorola), 1999-2000

This is part of a famous chart —you'll find out whose in a moment.

Go ahead and draw the longest valid lower trendline you can find on this chart.

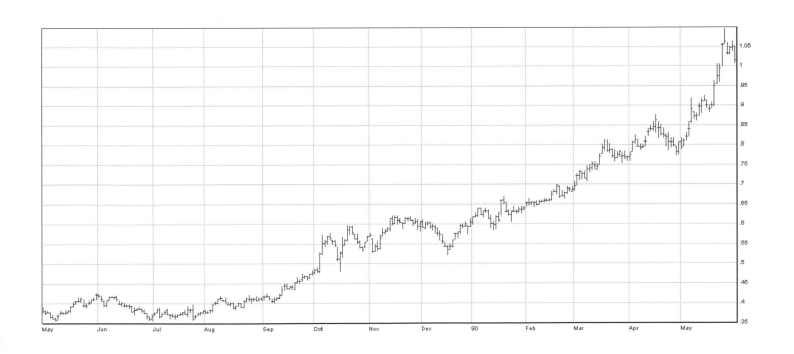

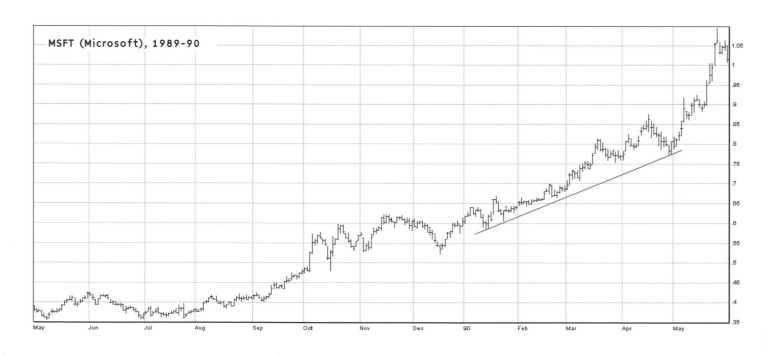

This is the chart for Microsoft during its incredible run-up: $1 invested in May 1989 was worth $2.70 only one year later.

You can see the stock accelerate in expectation of the release of Windows in May 1990, which took the PC market by storm. But the trend was visible long before.

MSFT (Microsoft), 1989-90

All stocks have a short code
or 'symbol'—Microsoft's is MSFT.

When you check a stock price
online, you'll need to know
its symbol.

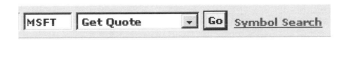

Wall Street professionals invent
pet names for some stocks.
Microsoft, for instance, is
sometimes referred to as "Mister
Softee" because of its symbol.

If you've found most of the
trendlines so far, you are well on
your way to forecasting stock
movements. Here's how.

First, draw the recent medium-
term trendlines, just as you have
been doing.

Next, extend the trendlines to the right of the chart, like this.

Now, whenever the chart approaches a trendline, the *most likely outcome* (remember those words) is for it to bounce off.

In this example, you would expect the chart to continue down until it meets the lower trendline and then bounce up.

Which is what happened here.

So the rule is this: when a chart approaches a trendline the *most likely outcome* is a bounce.

Let's walk through an example step-by-step. This is the chart for IBM in 2001-2002.

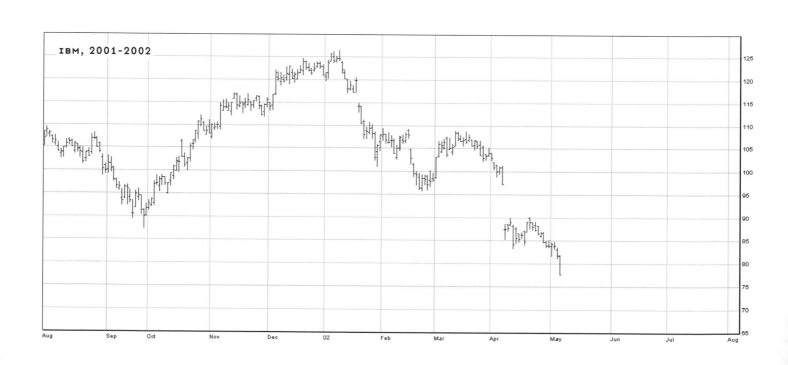

IBM, 2001-2002

First, draw on the most recent medium-term (more than one month) upper and lower trendlines.

There is also a recent short-term trendline here (we've drawn it with a dotted line)—since it's short-term, you can ignore it.

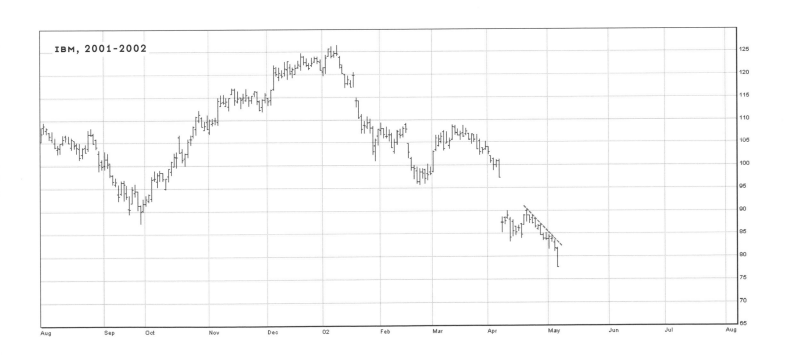

IBM, 2001-2002

This is what we drew. The lines aren't perfect, but they are good enough to forecast from.

Now we extend the trendlines…

IBM, 2001-2002

So what do you expect the next move to be?

(Hint: the rule is "when a chart approaches a trendline the most likely outcome is a bounce.")

IBM, 2001-2002

Since the chart is at the lower
trendline, the most likely next
move is to bounce up off it.

IBM, 2001-2002

And that is indeed what happened.

But we're not done with this chart.

What do you think the medium-term trend is?
(Hint: to find the medium-term trend, look at the medium-term trendlines.)

IBM, 2001-2002

Previous page

The medium-term trendlines slope downwards, so the medium-term trend is, most likely, down.

Since charts tend to bounce off trendlines, when caught between two of them, the chart will often follow the channel.

IBM, 2001-2002

So now we can say quite a bit about the chart we started with.

The trendlines tells us to expect a near-term bounce followed by a continuation downwards, in the channel.

IBM, 2001-2002

Which is precisely what
happened to IBM over the next
few months.

If you followed this reasoning,
you have just analyzed your
first chart.

Congratulations.

IBM, 2001-2002

Previous
page

Just think what you can do with
this insight.

IBM, 2001-2002

Trendlines are so powerful that some successful traders use them and nothing else to decide when to buy or sell.

(They are missing some tricks, as we'll see.)

IBM, 2001-2002

Let's try another.

First, draw the most recent
trendlines on this chart.

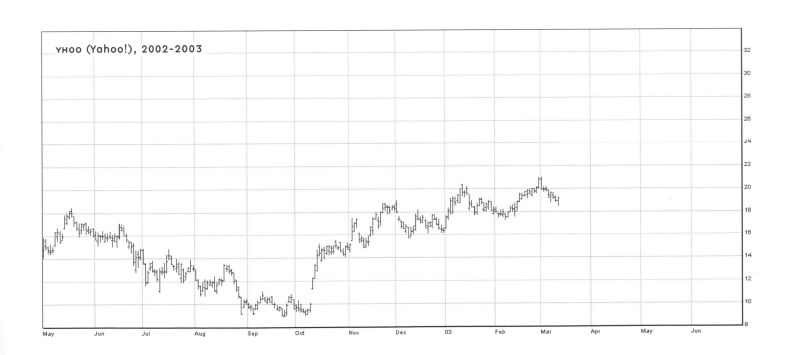

YHOO (Yahoo!), 2002-2003

There are a couple of alternative upper trendlines here. The one we chose (the solid line) has the advantage of being parallel to the lower line. But either one will work.

Now we extend the trendlines to the right.

YHOO (Yahoo!), 2002-2003

So what do you predict is the
most likely next move for
this stock?

YHOO (Yahoo!), 2002-2003

Up.

The chart is at the lower trendline: the most likely next move is a 'bounce' up off that line.

YHOO (Yahoo!), 2002-2003

So, would you buy or sell
this stock?

YHOO (Yahoo!), 2002-2003

In fact, the chart bounced right through the upper trendline.

If you decided to buy, you made nearly 30% profit over the next seven weeks.

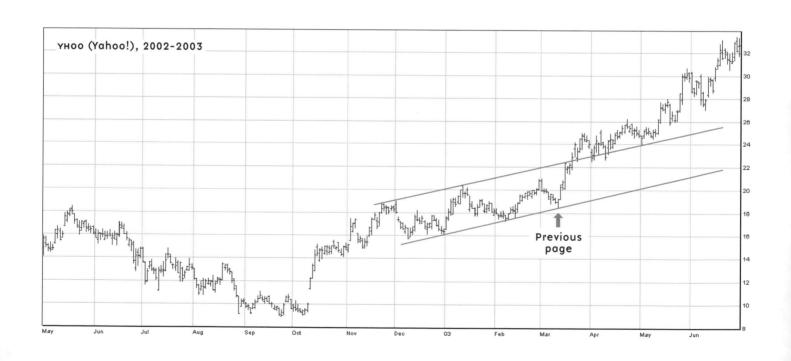

YHOO (Yahoo!), 2002-2003

Previous page

(Notice that the upper trendline turned into a rough lower trendline for the chart once it broke out of the channel. You'll see that happen a lot.)

YHOO (Yahoo!), 2002-2003

Upper trendline turns into...

...lower trendline

In a moment, we'll get back to Acme (finally). But first, you may be asking why bounces and channels should work at all?

No-one knows for sure, but here is the explanation favored by those who have researched the question...

YHOO (Yahoo!), 2002-2003

A stock price moves up for one
(and only one) reason: there is
more demand from people who
want to buy the stock than there
is supply from people who want
to sell it.

Buyers are driving the price up.

More demand
than supply

Likewise, prices move down for one (and only one) reason: more supply than demand.

More supply
than demand

If enough people believe the
price will bounce upwards from
a lower trend line, they
generate demand.

That demand causes the price
to bounce.

In other words, it's a
self-fulfilling prophecy:
the price bounces up because
enough people believe it will.

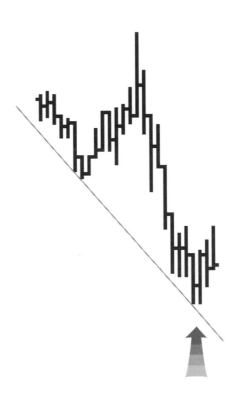

A channel, then, is a sort of tug of war between buyers and sellers.

In an up-sloping channel, the buyers are winning the tug of war. In a down-sloping channel, it's the sellers who have sentiment in their favor.

Sentiment can be a powerful thing. Down channels may continue down even after good news such as better than expected profits.

Since the price can't stay in a
channel forever, sooner or later
it has to break out. Which is
what happened in the chart for
Yahoo! we just looked at.

A breakout like this suggests a
winner in the tug of war
—in this case, the buyers.

As the losers accept defeat, there is often a significant move in the direction of the winners, as there was here.

It's almost as if the losers switch sides, so the upper trend line becomes a lower trend line.

Okay, now we're ready to get back to Acme. You own $100,000 of this stock and you have another $100,000 in cash. First draw in any trendline you consider to be a good one.

Remember this means:
- The most recent line
- With three or more touches
- Across more than one month.

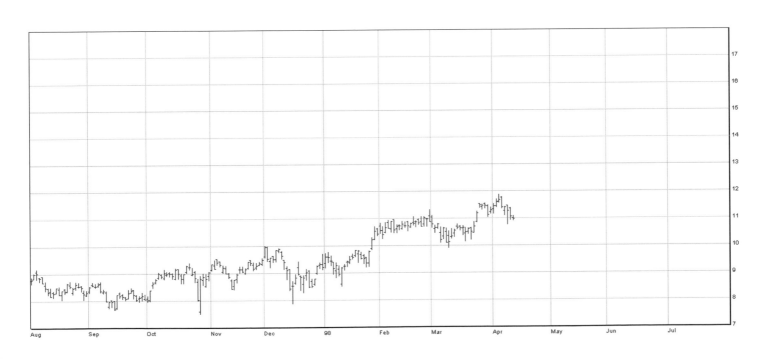

Two strong lines here, an upper
and a lower. Each has several
good touches.

Now choose one of these options
before flipping the page:
- Do nothing
- Buy $100,000 more stock
- Sell your $100,000 of stock.

A bounce off the lower trendline. Again, the chart bounced right through the upper trendline.

If you did nothing, you made $10,000 in seven weeks. If you bought more stock, you made $20,000. If you sold, you made nothing.

Previous page

Let's say you had decided to buy —what would you actually do to buy this stock?

You need to place the order with your broker either over the phone or online.

So what, exactly, do you say? Here's the first part of the conversation; pretty straightforward.

"Hi, this is Jane Doe, account number 123456, I'd like to place an order."

"Go ahead."

You

Your broker

This is how you give your order. It means you want to *buy* (say that with emphasis) 100 shares of Acme at whatever the price is when your order is filled (that's what "at the market" means).

Your broker repeats your order and gives you a ticket number, which is like a confirmation.

But you haven't actually bought the stock yet...

"Hi, this is Jane Doe, account number 123456, I'd like to place an order."

"Go ahead."

"I'd like to *buy* 100 Acme at the market."

"Correct."

"Buying 100 Acme at the market, correct?"

"Okay, your ticket number is 100100."

...When your broker says, "your order is filled," you have bought the stock.

It usually takes a minute (if it takes longer, your broker will offer to call you back when your order is filled).

Only now do you find out what you actually paid. That may seem a little strange; it's because the price is changing all the time.

"Hi, this is Jane Doe, account number 123456, I'd like to place an order."

"Go ahead."

"I'd like to buy 100 Acme at the market."

"Correct."

"Buying 100 Acme at the market, correct?"

"Okay, your ticket number is 100100."

(Long pause)

"Your order is filled. You bought 100 Acme at $11.00"

That's it. You just spent $11.00 x 100 = $1,100.

But hold on, you wanted to invest $100,000. To do that you would need to buy $100,000 divided by $11 = 9091 shares.

Typically, you would round that down to 9000 (in case the price goes up and you accidentally wind up spending more than you wanted). Odd? Maybe, but that's how it works.

"Hi, this is Jane Doe, account number 123456, I'd like to place an order."

"Go ahead."

"I'd like to buy 100 Acme at the market."

"Correct."

"Buying 100 Acme at the market, correct?"

"Okay, your ticket number is 10010."

(Long pause)

"Your order is filled. You bought 100 Acme at $11.00"

Now over to you.

You want to buy 1000 shares in Microsoft. You've already introduced yourself, what would you say to place the order?

"Hi, this is John Doe, account number 654321, I'd like to place an order."

"Go ahead."

Here's what you would say.

(If you wanted to sell, you just say "sell" instead of "buy" —everything else is the same.)

"Hi, this is John Doe, account number 654321, I'd like to place an order."

"Go ahead."

"I'd like to *buy* 1000 Microsoft at the market."

"Correct."

"Buying 1000 Microsoft at the market, correct?"

"Okay, your ticket number is 100101."

(Long pause)

"Your order is filled. You bought 1000 Microsoft at $26.88."

Back to the Acme chart. So now the upper trendline has been invalidated and the chart has returned to the lower trendline.

Assume you still have $100,000 of stock. What will you do now?
- Nothing
- Buy $100,000 more stock
- Sell your $100,000 of stock.

A strong bounce. Not bad.

If you did nothing, you made
$30,000. If you bought more
stock, you made $60,000.

Try finding a horizontal
trendline on this chart.

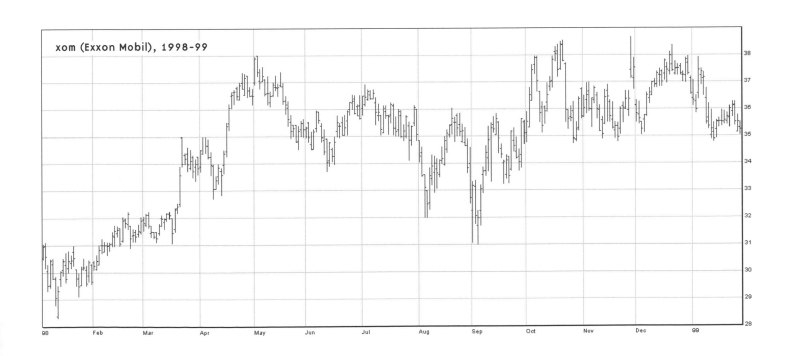

xom (Exxon Mobil), 1998-99

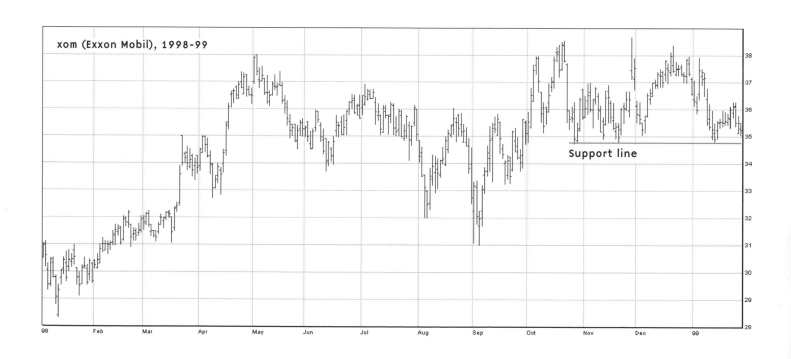

A horizontal line underneath a chart like this is called a 'support' line since it seems to support the price at that level.

(A horizontal line above a chart is called a 'resistance' line since it resists progress to higher levels.)

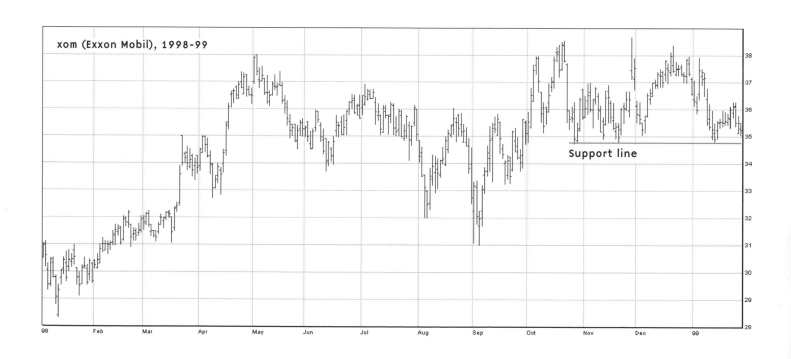

xom (Exxon Mobil), 1998-99

Support line

Draw a support line on this
chart and forecast the most
likely next move.

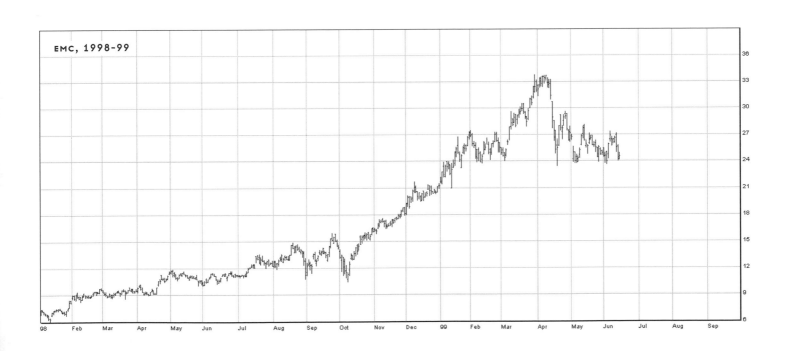

EMC, 1998-99

It bounces up off support.

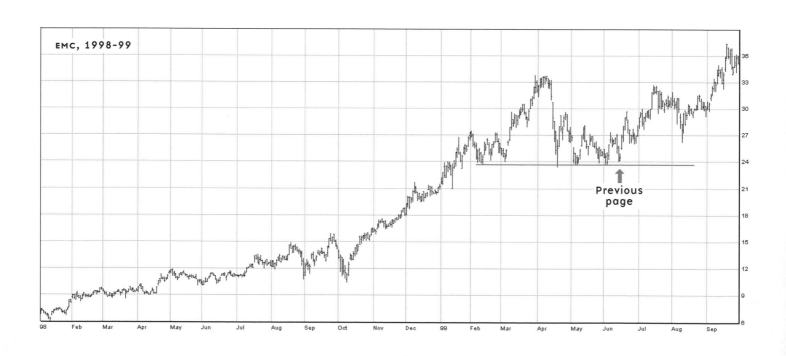

EMC, 1998-99

Previous
page

Support and resistance are stronger when they occur at round numbers like $30. Why? Perhaps because many investors use them as trigger points: "I'll sell if it ever falls to $30."

The Dow Jones Industrial Average ('the Dow' to friends) provides a famous example…

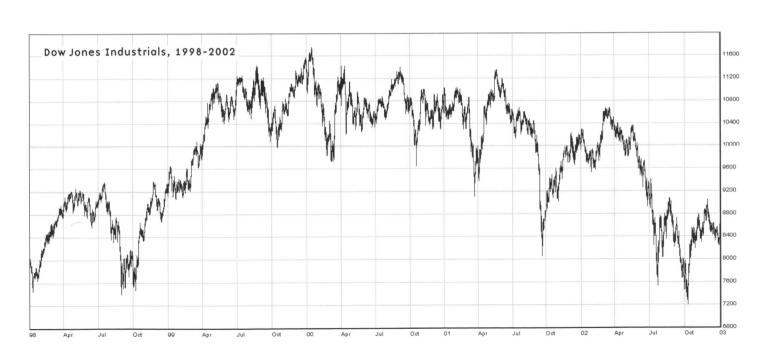

Dow Jones Industrials, 1998-2002

For three years it seemed to keep coming back to the 10,000 level, often hesitating there or changing direction.

(The Dow, incidentally, is an average of 30 big stocks chosen by the editors of the *Wall Street Journal*.)

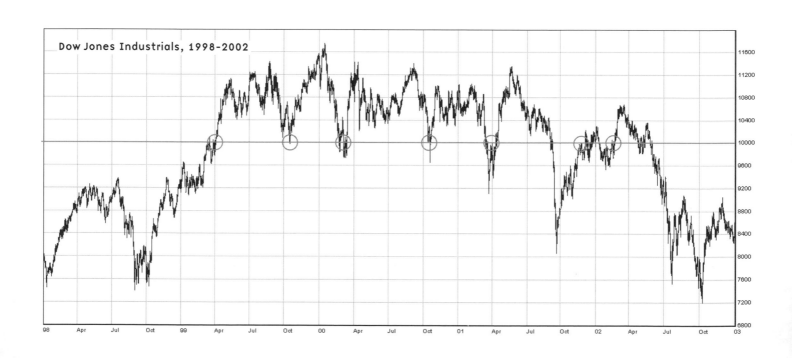

Dow Jones Industrials, 1998–2002

Another chart. What do you
think happens next?

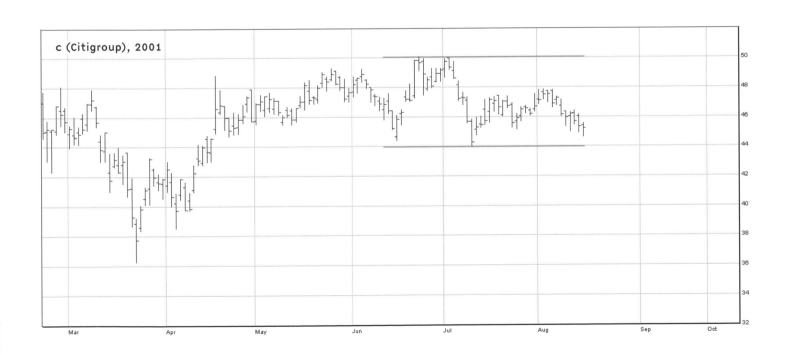

c (Citigroup), 2001

If you said "up" you may want to take a closer look at that support line.

It has only one touch. So it doesn't qualify as a support line at all.

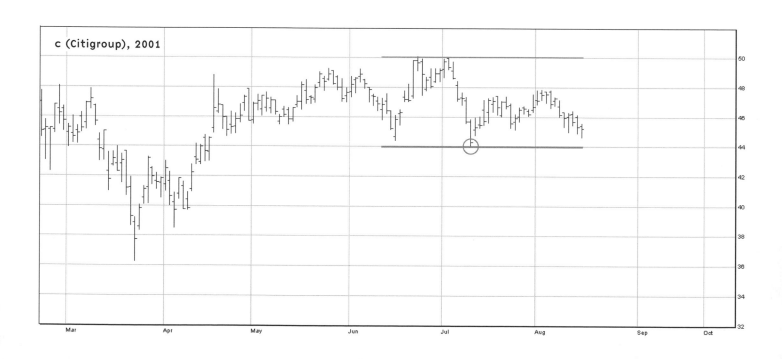

c (Citigroup), 2001

The resistance line isn't much better—the touches are spread over less than one month.

You really don't have much to go on for this chart. In that situation, which is very common, the best policy is to wait for more clarity.

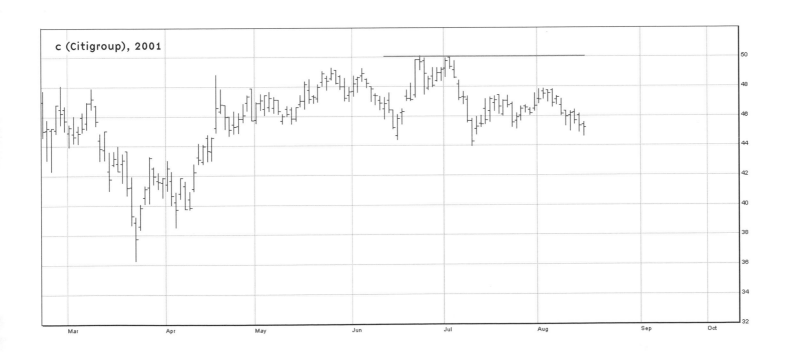

c (Citigroup), 2001

Here is what happened, a
nasty fall.

The lesson: make sure you have
good lines before basing
decisions on them.

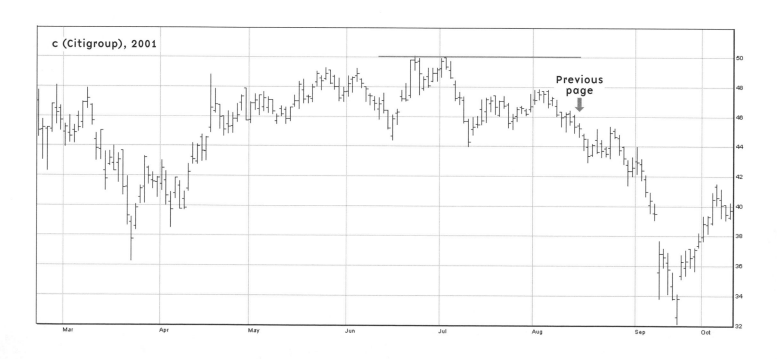

Let's recap what we've covered so far. Charts may have upper trendlines…

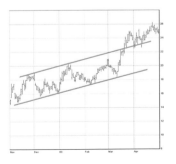

…lower trendlines…

…or both, forming a channel.

When it is horizontal, an upper trendline is called resistance…

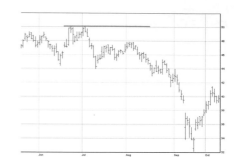

…and a lower horizontal trendline is called support.

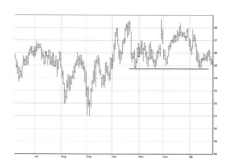

(When you have both at once, that's called a 'rectangle', but it's quite a rare pattern.)

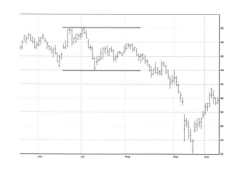

To qualify as a trendline, you need at least three good touches on the chart.

The more touches, the stronger the trendline.

(Support and resistance lines are also stronger at round numbers like $50.)

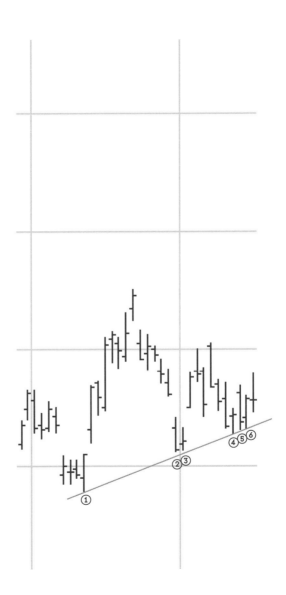

Prices are more likely to bounce off a trendline than to pass through it.

So, when there are two parallel trendlines, the chart will tend to move down the channel.

Got it? Okay, let's put all this together for the finale to Sequence One…

You own $100,000 of PFE, whose chart is below. Decide whether to:
- Hold the stock you have
- Buy $100,000 more stock
- Sell the stock you have.

Be sure to draw a trendline and decide what you would do before flipping the page.

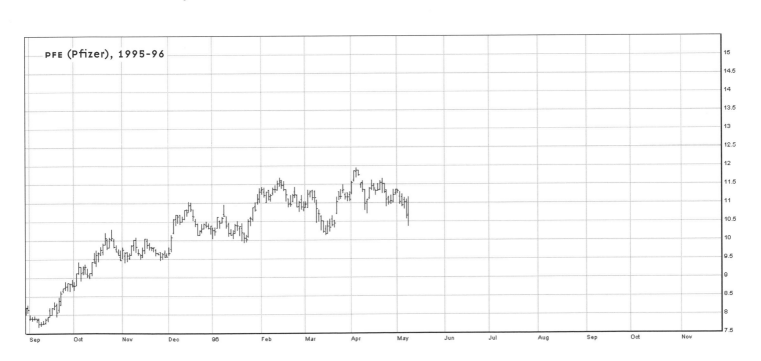

PFE (Pfizer), 1995-96

Either of these lower trendlines reveals a medium-term rising trend for Pfizer.

If you held, you made $37,000 in six months. If you bought more stock, you made $74,000. If you sold, you made nothing.

PFE (Pfizer), 1995-96

Previous page

A different stock but the same question. Again, assume you own $100,000 of this stock and $100,000 in cash.

Will you:
- Hold the stock you have for several months
- Buy $100,000 more stock
- Sell the stock you have?

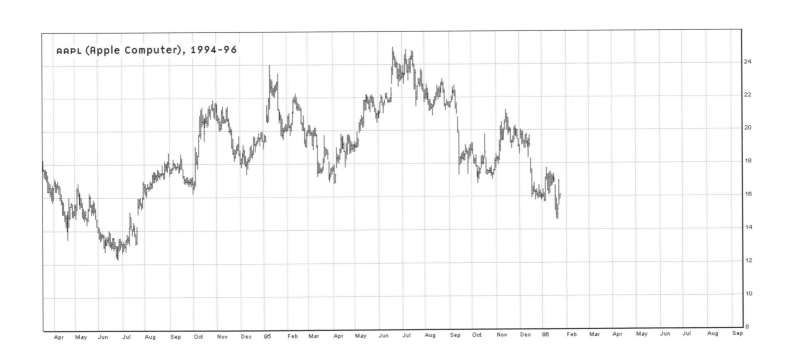

AAPL (Apple Computer), 1994-96

Tough times at Apple Computer. John Sculley had gone and Steve Jobs did not return until 1997. But all you needed to read the situation was the chart.

If you held, you lost $35,000 in seven months. If you bought more stock, you lost $70,000. If you sold, you lost nothing.

AAPL (Apple Computer), 1994-96

Previous page

Let's say you decided to sell 6000 shares of Apple Computer. How would you place that order with your broker?

"Hi, this is John Doe,
account number 654321,
I'd like to place an order."

"Go ahead."

"I'd like to *sell* 6000 Apple
Computer at the market."

"Selling 6000 Apple at the
market, correct?"

"Correct."

"Okay, your ticket number is
100102."

(Long pause)

"Your order is filled. You
sold 6000 Apple Computer
at $16.12."

Finally, imagine you own
$100,000 of INTC in late 1999.

Will you:
- Hold
- Buy $100,000 more
- Sell?

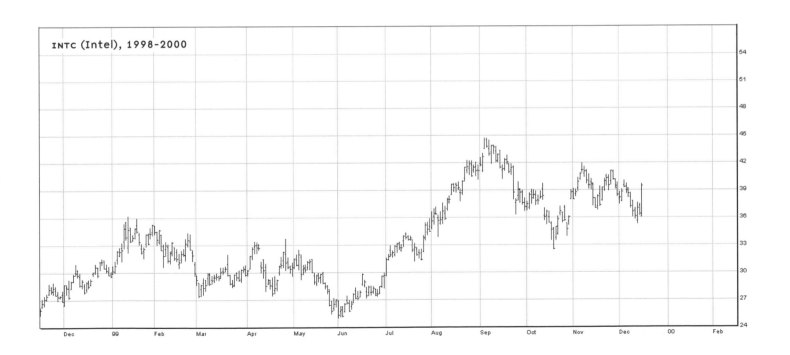

INTC (Intel), 1998-2000

The trendlines give conflicting signals. We'll learn how to deal with this situation in Sequence Two.

If you held, you made $42,000 in two months. If you bought more stock, you made $84,000. If you sold, you made nothing.

INTC (Intel), 1998-2000

Previous page

How did you do?

If you made money overall, congratulations!

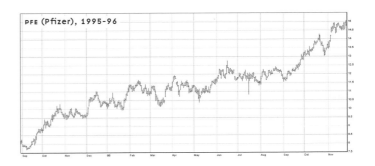

PFE (Pfizer), 1995-96

AAPL (Apple Computer), 1994-96

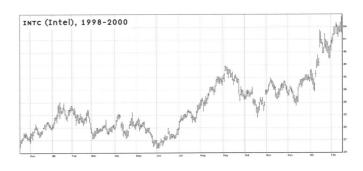

INTC (Intel), 1998-2000

But your new skills will fade unless you try them out on real charts within a week.

(There is a list of places to find charts in the Next Steps section on page 229.)

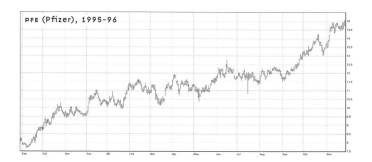

PFE (Pfizer), 1995-96

AAPL (Apple Computer), 1994-96

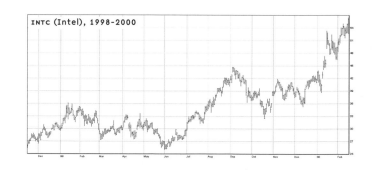

INTC (Intel), 1998-2000

You don't have to trade for real, of course, and certainly not for $100,000 (that was just to make things interesting). There's more to learn about charts first.

All you need to do is print out a real chart, draw on it, make a forecast, and see if you are right over the next few days.

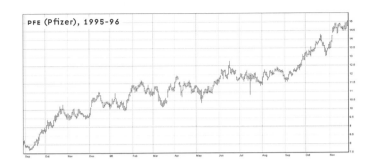

PFE (Pfizer), 1995-96

AAPL (Apple Computer), 1994-96

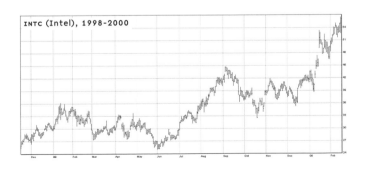

INTC (Intel), 1998-2000

Have fun.

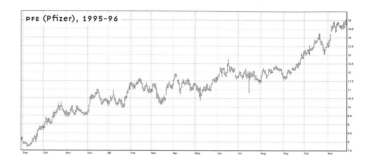

PFE (Pfizer), 1995-96

AAPL (Apple Computer), 1994-96

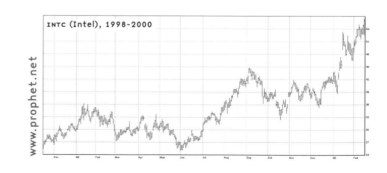

INTC (Intel), 1998-2000

www.prophet.net

Pause point

To get the most from this book, you should pause after reading this page.

There's much more to come—but be sure to stop here and return to the book a few days later. Here's why.

In the days after you learn something new, your memory fades. You may forget most of what you learned. That might seem annoying, but if you remembered everything you had seen only once, your memory would quickly get overcrowded.

So how do you prevent fading? You need to reinforce what you want to remember. The best way to reinforce knowledge is simple: use it. That's why we recommend practicing on real stock charts over the next few days.

Then come back to *Stikky Stock Charts* and start at Sequence Two on the page after this one.

(We have noticed that, when readers continue straight on to Sequence Two, they often get stuck and don't complete it, or find that they forget what they have learned more quickly.)

If you are away from the book for more than a week, or if you don't get a chance to practice in between, you will want to review the end of Sequence One before starting Sequence Two.

When you're ready to continue, read from the next page to the **Pause point** at the end of Sequence Two on page 193.

And remember your promise: when asked a question in the text you will not flip ahead without attempting to answer it.

Sequence Two

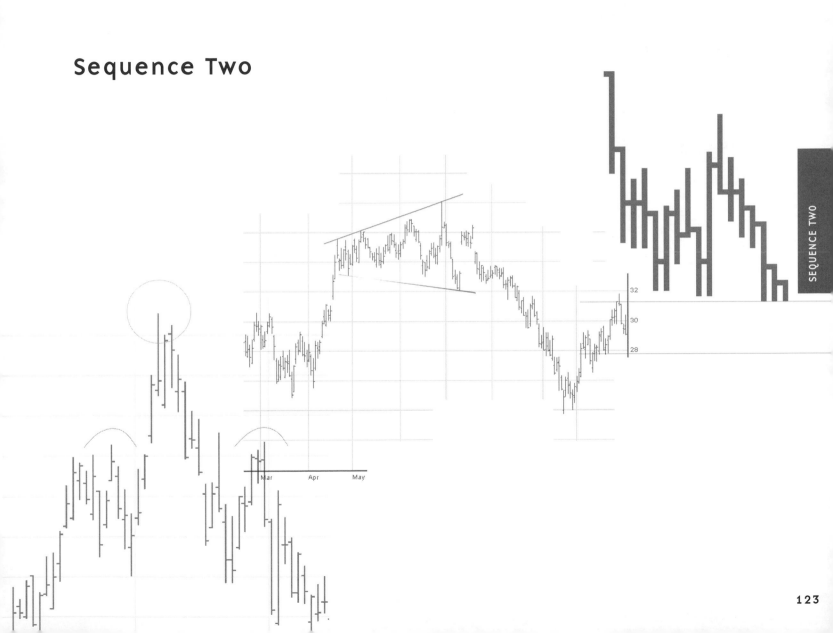

Mar   Apr   May

32

30

28

The first person to publish the theory that stock charts could be used to predict future prices was Charles Dow, of Dow Jones fame, in 1900.

Dow provided a theory but no proof. (Nothing wrong with that, of course, Einstein did the same thing five years later.)

Charles Dow

But Dow's theory began to attract cranks. For instance, people who believed that prices obey a ratio discovered by a 13th century mathematician from Pisa, Italy, called Leonardo Fibonacci ("fib-o-NAH-chee").

No sensible explanation was offered for why this might be.

Thanks to the cranks, serious researchers steered clear of chartism until…

Leonardo Fibonacci

...2000, when Professor Andrew Lo of MIT examined hundreds of stock charts over a 31-year period.

To the surprise of many, he found a small number of chart patterns that provide information about future prices.

It is Lo's patterns we look at in this sequence.

Andrew Lo, MIT

But first a brief recap.

Draw a trendline on this chart
and forecast the most likely
next move.

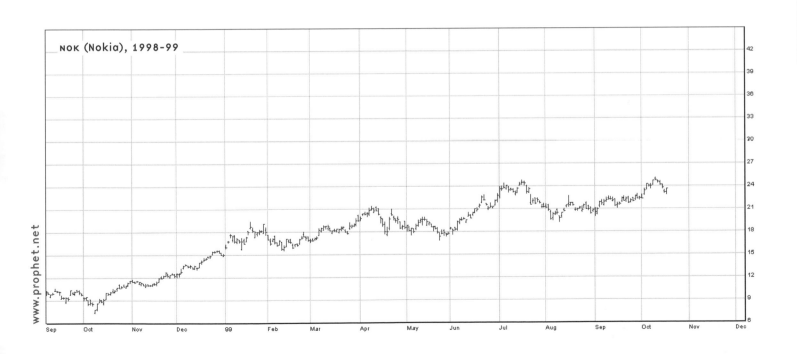

NOK (Nokia), 1998-99

www.prophet.net

Up. This is the rise of Finnish cellphone maker Nokia. (They are listed on the New York Stock Exchange along with hundreds of other foreign companies.)

NOK tripled in 1999, so you could have been forgiven for thinking you had missed out on the move. You hadn't; it carried on up to $62.50.

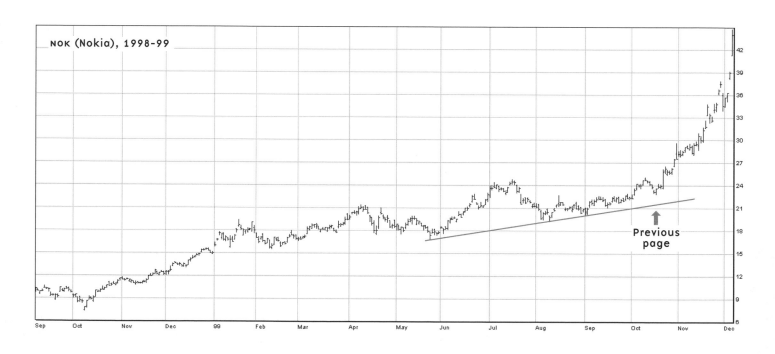

NOK (Nokia), 1998-99

Previous page

Draw trendlines for the part of this chart just before September 11, 2001. Then draw any trendlines you can find for the chart after 9-11.

AMR (American Airlines), 2001-2002

Volume (Millions)

Did you find these lines?

You can see that American Airlines' stock was unsteady even before 9-11.

And the uncertainty afterwards led to these contradictory trends, making it difficult to forecast what will follow.

AMR (American Airlines), 2001-2002

Volume (Millions)

A clue, though, is in the volume chart shown here below the main chart. Most chart sources can do this for you.

It shows the number of shares traded each day. A tall bar means a lot of shares were traded; a short bar means fewer shares were traded.

AMR (American Airlines), 2002

You can use the volume bars to see the strength of each side in the tug of war between buyers and sellers.

Here's how. Rising volume (bars getting taller) means there is confidence in whatever the stock chart is doing at that point —it is a strong trend.

For instance, volume is rising in April, when the stock chart moves down. So the downward trend is strong.

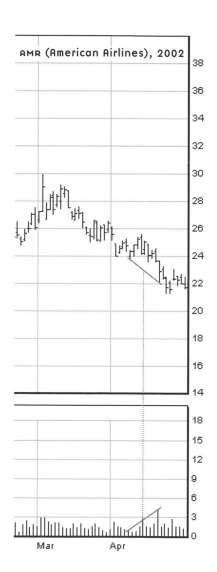

AMR (American Airlines), 2002

Similarly, falling volume (bars getting shorter) means there is little confidence in whatever the stock chart is doing at that point—it is a weak trend.

The falling volume in March, when the stock chart moves up, suggests that the upward trend is weak.

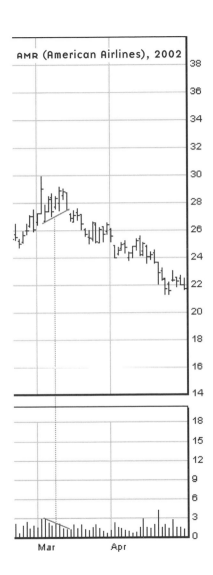

AMR (American Airlines), 2002

So we have evidence that the down trend is strong and the up trend is weak.

In other words, the sellers are the stronger team, likely to take this stock lower.

And they were: in the next six months AMR plummeted from $22 to $4.

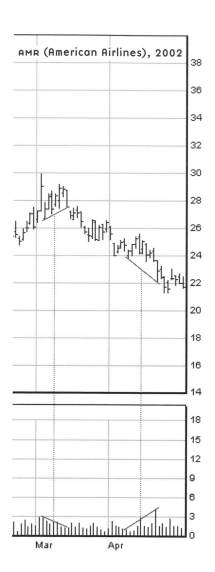

AMR (American Airlines), 2002

TWO

Time for some new patterns. As we've seen, sometimes trendlines are parallel, forming rectangles or channels like these.

But sometimes they aren't parallel...

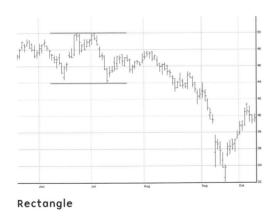

Rectangle

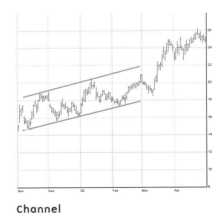

Channel

When lines are broadening, we have what practitioners call a 'megaphone'.

Broadening trendlines suggest growing disagreement between buyers and sellers—it's like everyone is shouting at once.

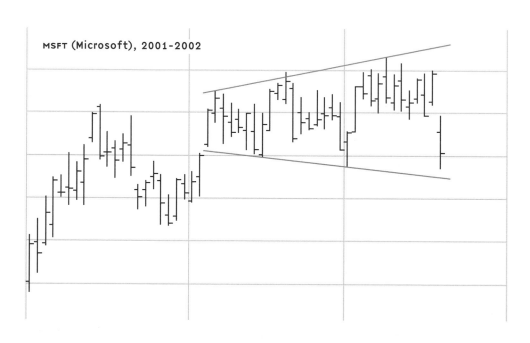

MSFT (Microsoft), 2001-2002

Disagreement is not normally a good sign: if it occurs after an uptrend, the most likely next move is down.

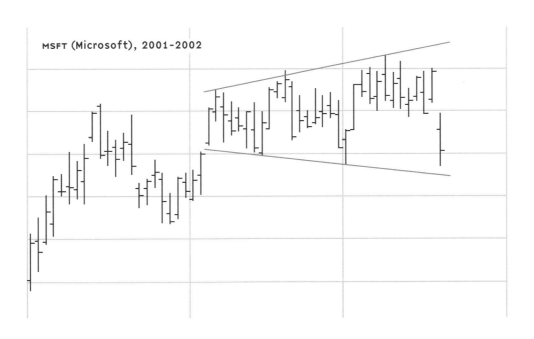

MSFT (Microsoft), 2001–2002

When trendlines are narrowing, we have a 'triangle'.

Let's look at these three types of triangle pattern more closely to see what is going on.

Ascending triangle

Descending triangle

Symmetrical triangle

When one line is horizontal and the other slopes upwards, we have an 'ascending triangle'.

It looks like the buyers (the up-sloping line) are stronger than the sellers (the flat line). So the most likely outcome is for the buyers to win and the price to move up.

MSFT (Microsoft), 1997

When one line is horizontal and the other slopes downwards, we have a 'descending triangle'.

Here the sellers (the down-sloping line) are more assertive than the buyers (the flat line). So the most likely outcome is for the sellers to win and the price to move down.

MSFT (Microsoft), 1995-96

And when we have both an up-sloping and a down-sloping trendline, this is known as a 'symmetrical triangle'.

The breakout from a symmetrical triangle could go either way, as its name implies.

GSK (GlaxoSmithKline), 1997

Here are the four again.

As you will remember, a good trendline has at least three touches of the chart, as all these lines do.

Poorly trained chartists who break this rule wind up seeing patterns where there aren't any.

Ascending triangle

Symmetrical triangle

Descending triangle

Megaphone

Now let's look at how these patterns appear in full charts. There is an ascending triangle in this chart. Your task is to find it and draw it on.

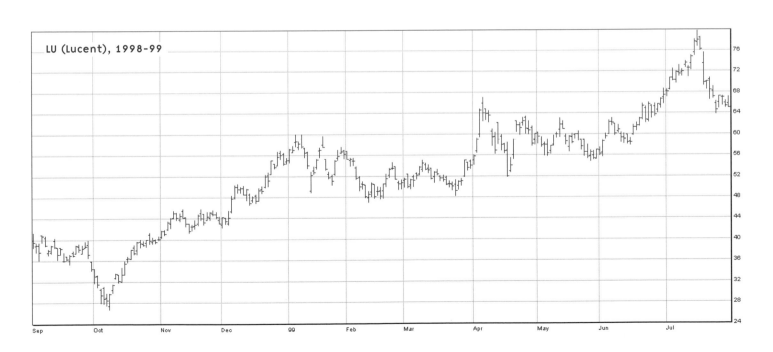

This is a bit more difficult than what we have looked at so far, so take your time.

LU (Lucent), 1998-99

An *ascending* triangle often precedes a move *up*, as it did here.

A pattern that suggests a move up is called a 'bullish' pattern.

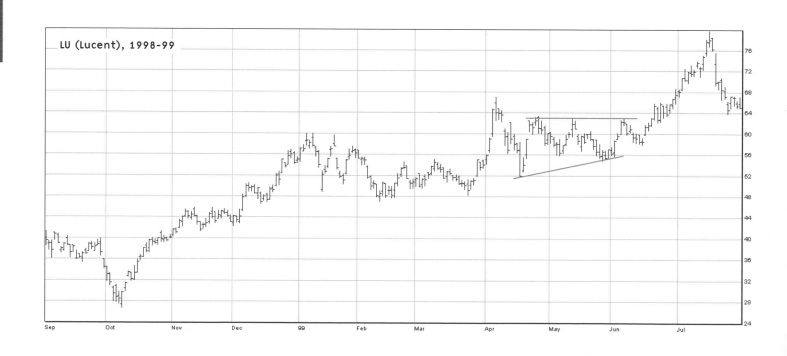

LU (Lucent), 1998-99

There is a descending triangle
in this chart for Amazon.com.
Try to find it.

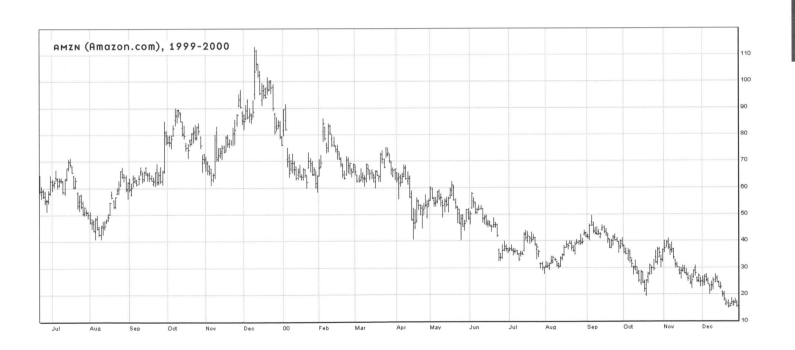

AMZN (Amazon.com), 1999-2000

Descending triangles suggest a possible move *down*, as you can see in this dramatic decline for Amazon.com.

A pattern that suggests a move down is called a 'bearish' pattern.

AMZN (Amazon.com), 1999-2000

Which one of the four patterns can you find near the end of this chart?

(It may help to turn back to page 142 to remind yourself of the patterns. Notice that they all unfold over a few months, not more.)

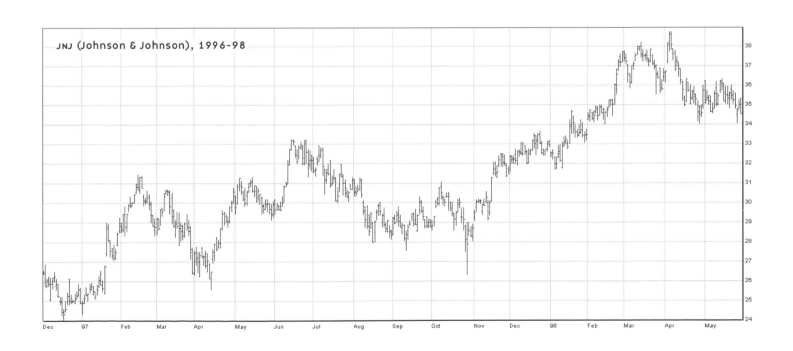

JNJ (Johnson & Johnson), 1996-98

A megaphone.  Remember, broadening lines mean everyone shouting at once: megaphone.

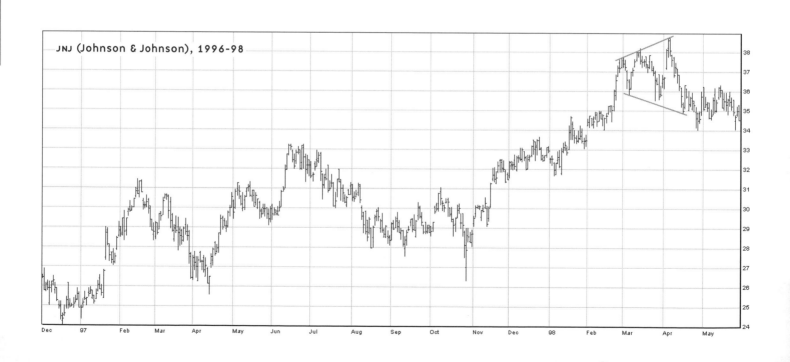

JNJ (Johnson & Johnson), 1996-98

For these next charts, decide which way you think the market will go next.

Is the market here more likely to go up, go down, or neither?

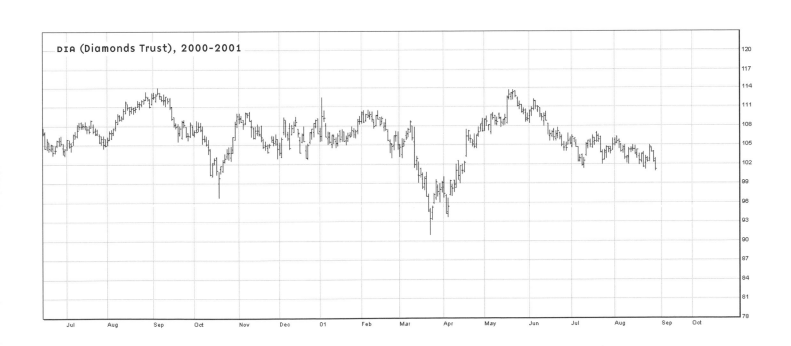

DIA (Diamonds Trust), 2000-2001

A descending triangle (with two support lines, just to make sure), suggesting a move down.

DIA, known as 'diamonds', is a stock designed to track the Dow Jones Industrials index.

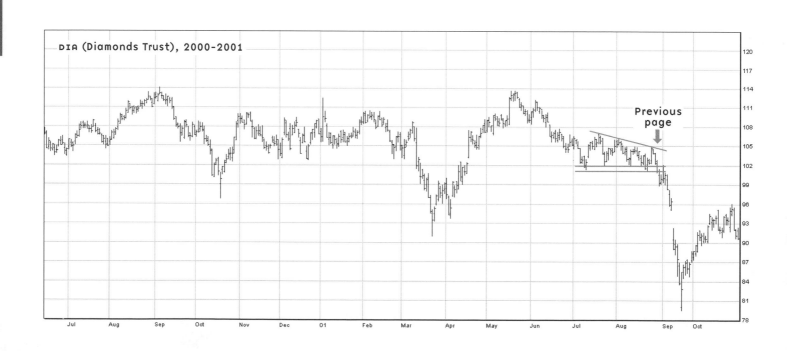

DIA (Diamonds Trust), 2000–2001

Previous page

Find a pattern in the most
recent few months of this chart
and say what you think is the
most likely next move.

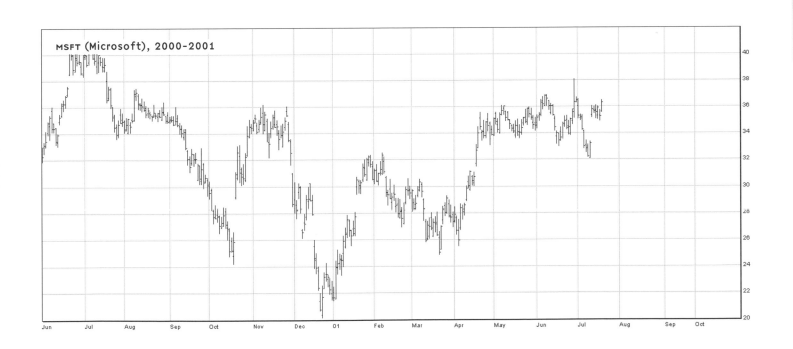

MSFT (Microsoft), 2000-2001

A megaphone, suggesting a downward move. To the uninitiated, the chart may have looked like it would continue upwards.

Of course, sometimes the uninitiated are right, and you will lose money. There are two things you can do about this.

MSFT (Microsoft), 2000-2001

Previous page

The first is to wait for a breakout to confirm direction. Let's see how in this chart for AOL.

Draw the pattern that has formed in the last few months of this chart.

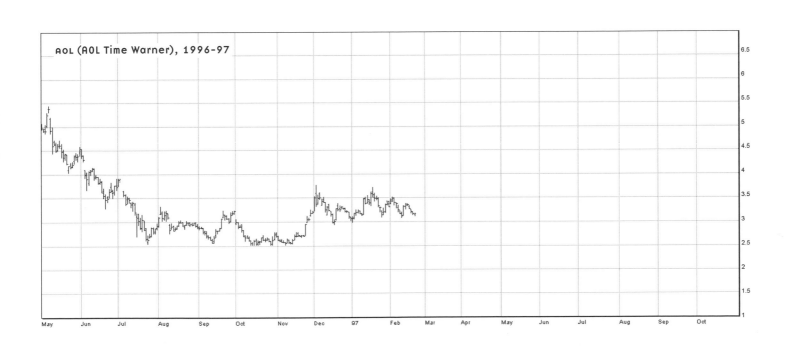

AOL (AOL Time Warner), 1996–97

A symmetrical triangle, which could go either way.

So we wait for a breakout…

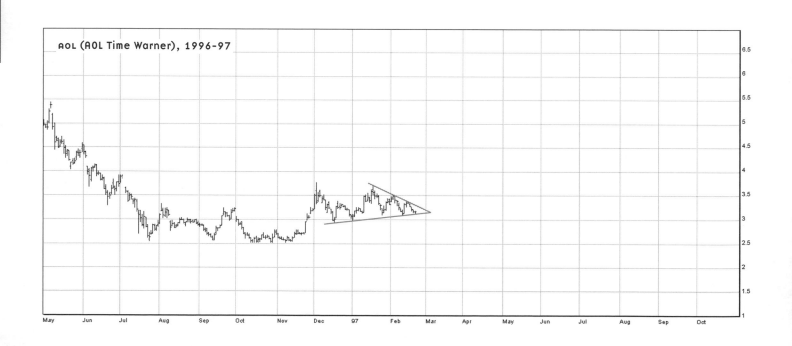

AOL (AOL Time Warner), 1996-97

This is what unfolds over the next three days.

Look closely. What is your view now: a move up or down?

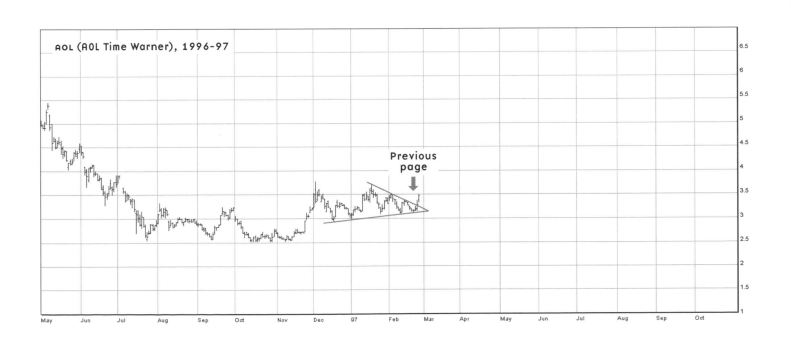

AOL (AOL Time Warner), 1996-97

Previous page

TWO

Since the chart broke the upper trendline, a move up was the most likely outcome.

And that move turned out to be the start of a major upward trend.

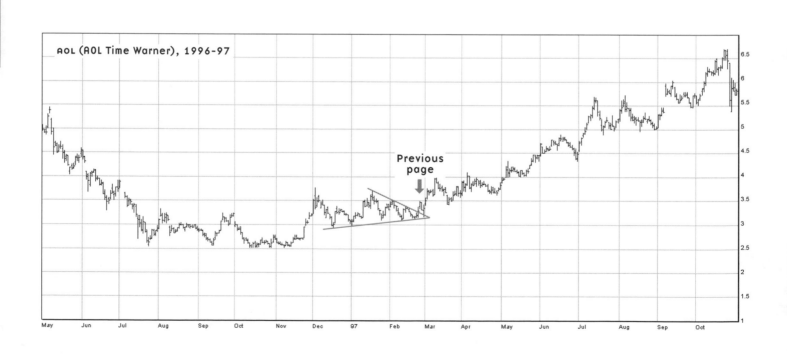

AOL (AOL Time Warner), 1996-97

Previous page

The second thing you can do to minimize losses—and perhaps the most important concept in this book—is to set a 'stop loss'.

A stop loss is the dollar amount you are prepared to lose before giving up on a trade.

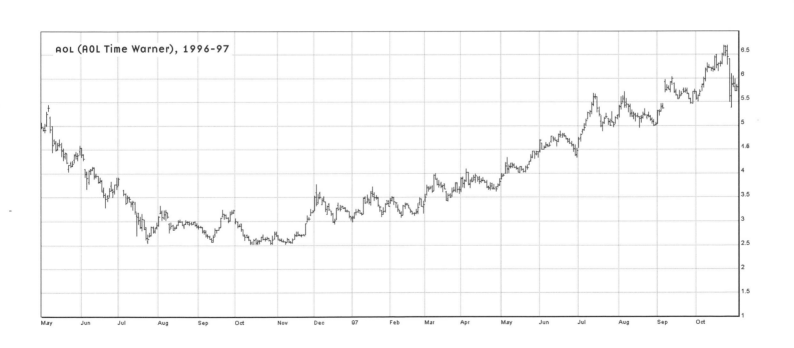

AOL (AOL Time Warner), 1996-97

Setting a stop loss is simple.

You decide how much you are willing to lose if the trade goes in the wrong direction —$500, say.

Then, as soon as the loss gets to $500, you sell.
(Most brokers will do this automatically for you if you ask for a stop loss order.)

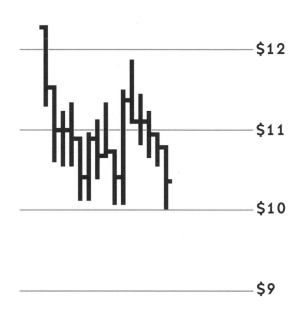

$12

$11

$10

$9

Here's an example. This stock
has fallen to a support line at
$10 (a nice round number) and
you are expecting a bounce.

Let's say you buy 500 shares at
$10—①.

At the same time you place a
stop loss order $1 below—②.

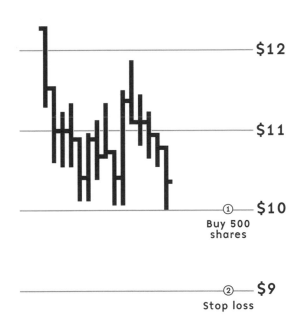

$12

$11

① $10
Buy 500
shares

② $9
Stop loss

Now if the market moves down through $9, your stock will be sold automatically. You will have lost 500 x $1 = $500.

Even if the market continues down, your loss is limited to $500, since you are out of the market.

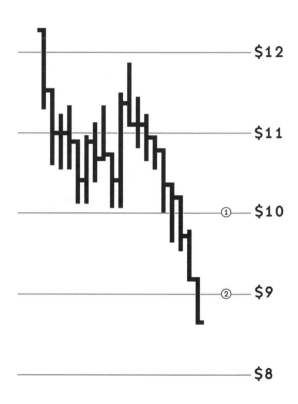

If you hadn't set a stop loss, you may be tempted to stay in the game, *which is exactly how investors the world over lose their money.*

And it's how professionals make theirs—profiting from those who can't bring themselves to get out of a losing position (often in a stock they have become emotionally attached to).

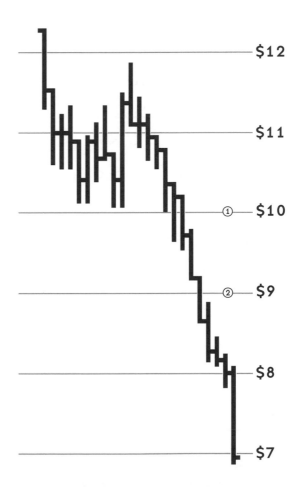

If you learn only one thing today, make it this: when a trade turns sour, *get out*.

In fact, you should expect this to happen for about half the positions you enter. Profitable traders experience many small losses and a few big wins.

It turns out that the secret of locking in those wins, when they come, is also the stop loss…

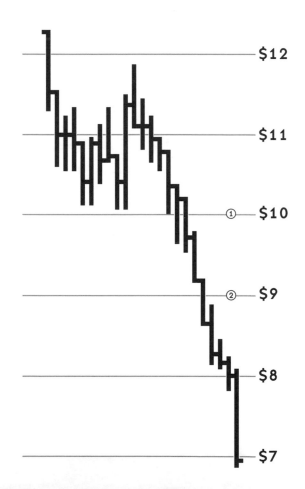

Let's say that, instead of falling, the stock you bought climbs to $12—③.

Now you can move your stop loss up as well, so that it stays $1 under the price—④.

(Moving a stop loss up is optional, but never, never move one down: you're extending your losses.)

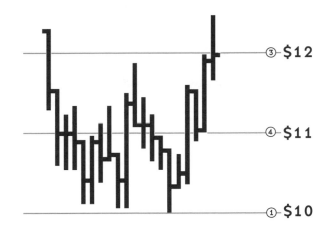

③-$12

④-$11

①-$10

②-$9

If the market falls back, your stop loss is triggered and you keep the profit up to that point.

In this case, you sell automatically at $11, for a $500 profit.

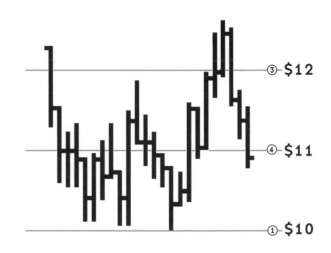

③-$12

④-$11

①-$10

②-$9

Your turn.

You've decided to buy 500 shares at $20. If the maximum you are prepared to lose on this trade is $500, where would you place the stop loss?

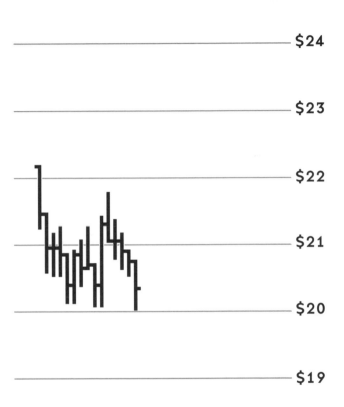

$19.

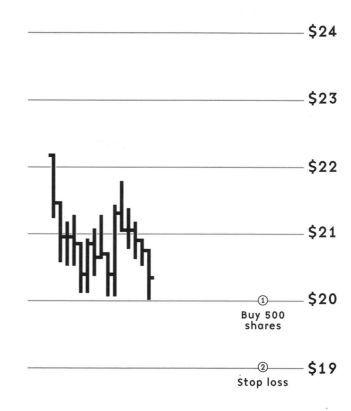

$24

$23

$22

$21

$20
① Buy 500
shares

$19
② Stop loss

If the stock climbs to $24, what would you do with the stop loss?

You could move it up to $23, locking in $3 of profit per share.

If you are unsure about stop losses, now is a good time to go back and review the last few pages.

Okay, back to patterns. Two more and then we'll put it all together.

These two patterns commonly mark the top of a trend. In other words, if you see them after an uptrend, the most likely next move is down.

Let's take a closer look at them.

Double top

Head and shoulders top

A 'double top' forms when an up-trending chart…

…first fails to match the last high…

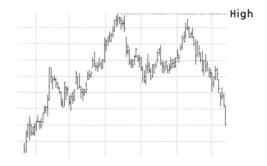

…and then drops lower than the valley between the two highs.

IBM, 1999

TWO

A 'head and shoulders' top
occurs when an uptrend...

...forms a lower high, making
the shoulder-head-shoulder
pattern...

...and then drops below the
neckline between the two
shoulders.

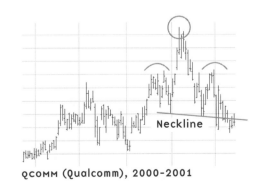

QCOMM (Qualcomm), 2000-2001

These patterns are only fully formed *when the chart drops below* the valley (for a double top) or neckline (for a head and shoulders top).

No drop, no top, you might say.

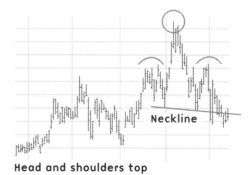

Double top

Head and shoulders top

Draw on this chart whichever
'top' pattern you discern.

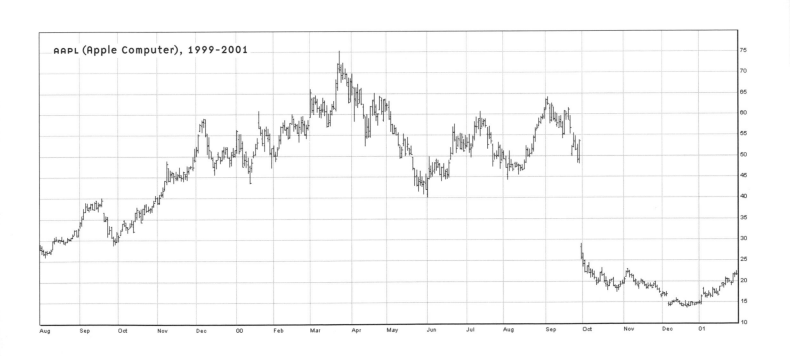

AAPL (Apple Computer), 1999-2001

A head and shoulders top.

Notice that the neckline slopes
so that it took a long time to
break.

AAPL (Apple Computer), 1999-2001

In what direction would you
expect this chart to move next?

SUNW (Sun Microsystems), 1999-2001

Down. This is a double top.

Notice, though, that the chart attempted (and failed) to form a new high after the double top —quite a common follow-up to a double top.

SUNW (Sun Microsystems), 1999-2001

Previous page

So now, for the grand finale, back to your imaginary portfolio.

You own $100,000 of BUBB and $100,000 cash.

Here is the recent chart for BUBB.

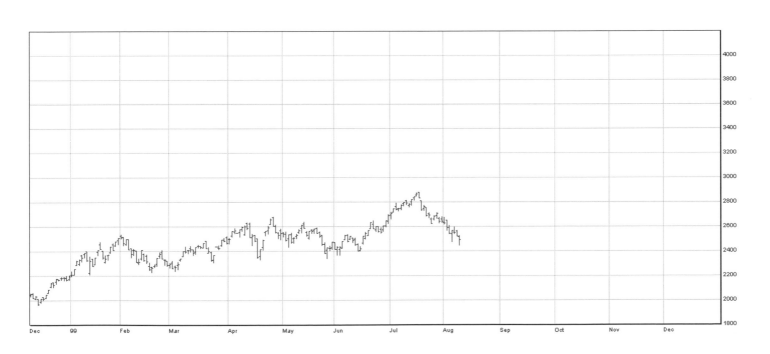

You are now armed with knowledge of trendlines, support and resistance, stop losses, volume, and these eight patterns.

If you had a particular difficulty with anything so far, you may want to go back and review it now.

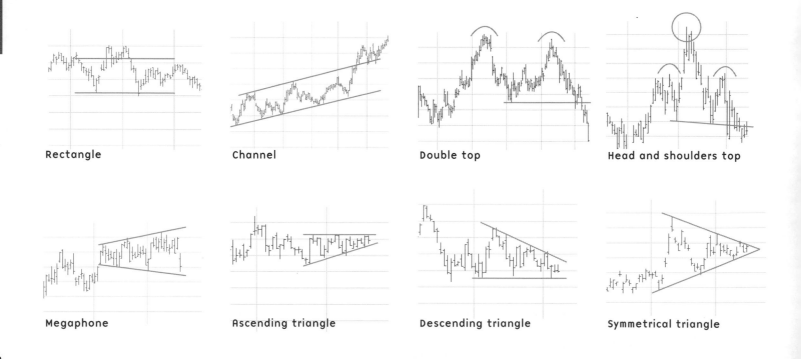

Rectangle

Channel

Double top

Head and shoulders top

Megaphone

Ascending triangle

Descending triangle

Symmetrical triangle

Take a good look at the chart.

When you are ready, decide whether to:
- Do nothing
- Buy $100,000 more BUBB
- Sell the $100,000 of BUBB that you own.

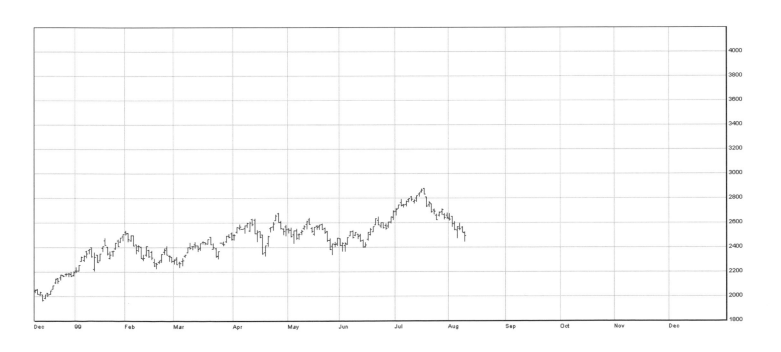

A solid uptrend continued.

If you did nothing, you made
$45,000 in the next seven
months. If you bought more
BUBB, you made $90,000.

If you sold, you made nothing.

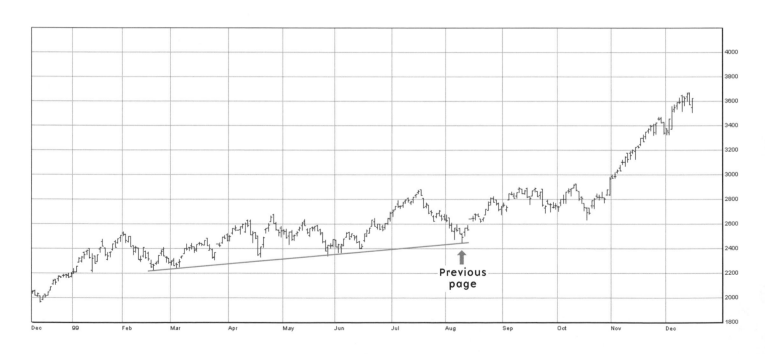

We zoomed out a little. Now it's just before the end of the year; what will you do? Assume, for simplicity, that the situation is still that you own $100,000 of BUBB and $100,000 cash.

Your choices again are:
- Do nothing
- Buy $100,000 more BUBB
- Sell the $100,000 of BUBB.

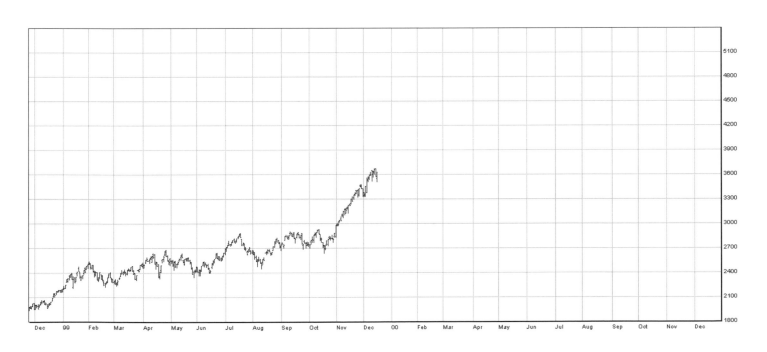

No patterns here, just the uptrend.

If you did nothing, you made $15,000 in four months. If you bought more BUBB, you made $30,000. If you sold, you made nothing.

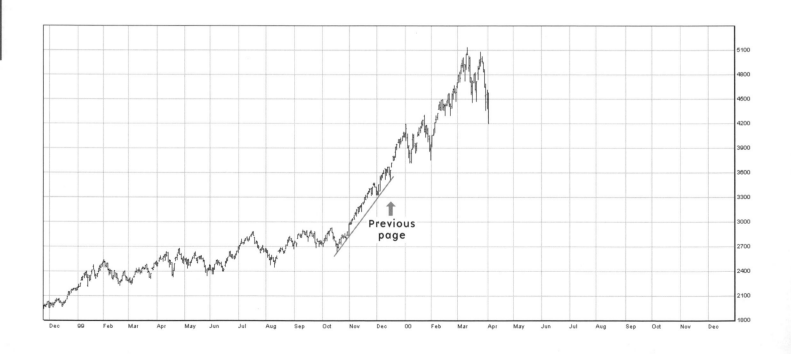

Previous page

What will you do now?

Same choices:
- Do nothing
- Buy $100,000 more BUBB
- Sell the $100,000 of BUBB.

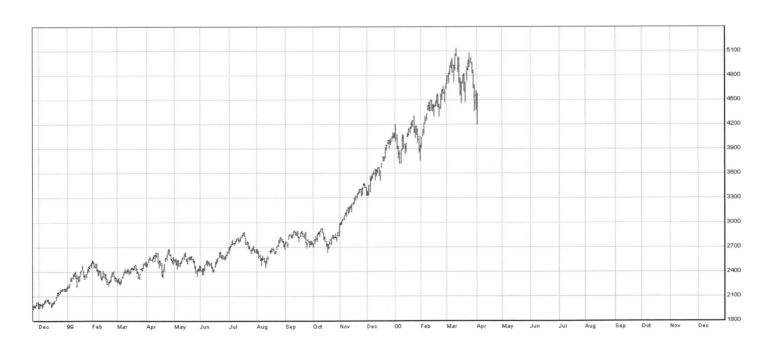

This is a double top. The market had already dropped below the lowest point in the valley between the two tops.

If you did nothing, you lost $20,000 in four months. If you bought more BUBB, you lost $40,000. If you sold, you lost nothing.

Last decision.

What will you do now:
- Nothing
- Buy $100,000 more BUBB
- Sell the $100,000 of BUBB?

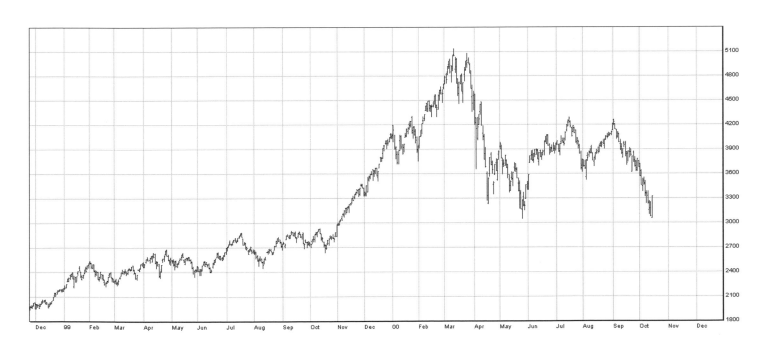

Another double top, followed by a strong downtrend. In fact, if you look closely, you can see a third double top here.

If you did nothing, you lost $30,000 in three months. If you bought more BUBB, you lost $60,000. If you sold, you lost nothing.

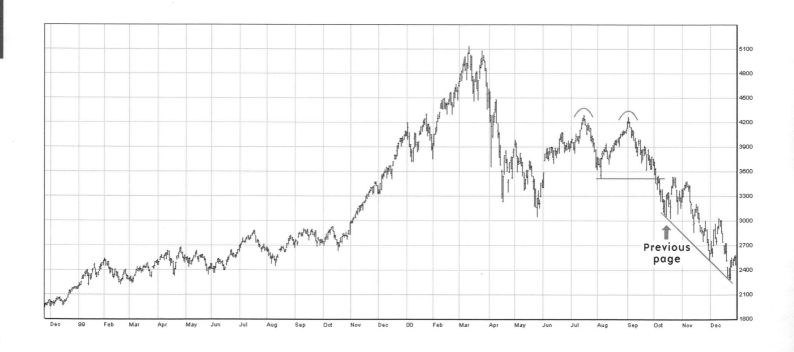

Previous page

How did you do overall?

If you made money, you are on
your way to being a technical
analyst.

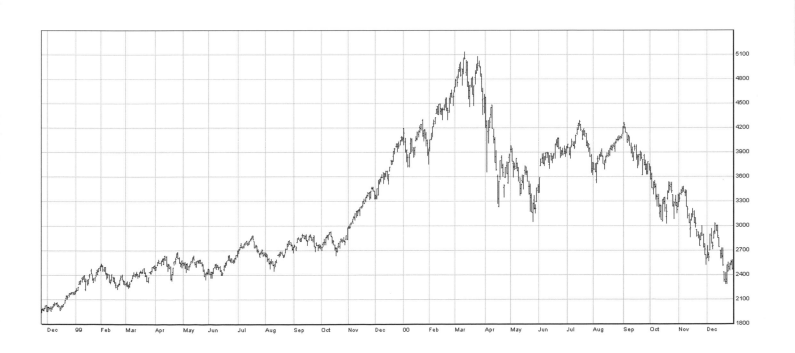

Incidentally, if you had sold the stock back in August 1999 and left $200,000 in the bank, you would have made $11,500 interest over this period.

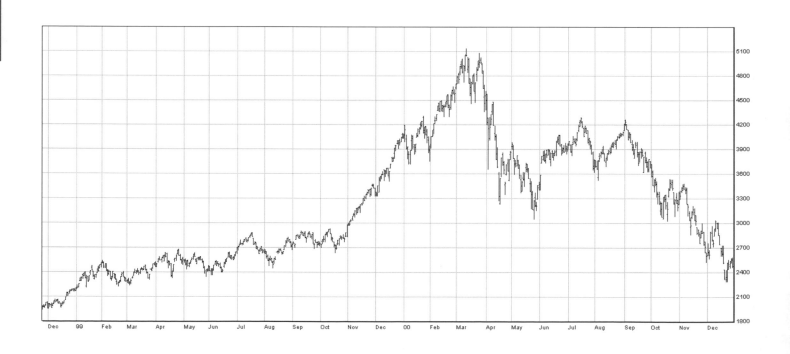

And if you had done nothing
about your inheritance—left
$100,000 in BUBB , $100,000 in
the bank—you would still have
made money, but only $5,000.

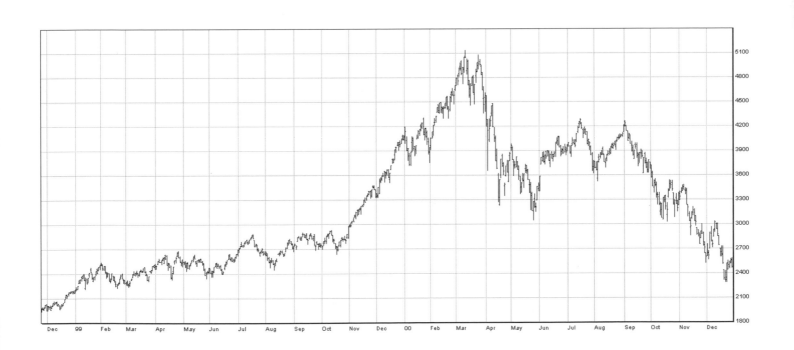

You may be interested to know that this is a real chart—it is the roller coaster ride of the NASDAQ from late 1998 to the end of 2001.

It is, in fact, a classic bubble.

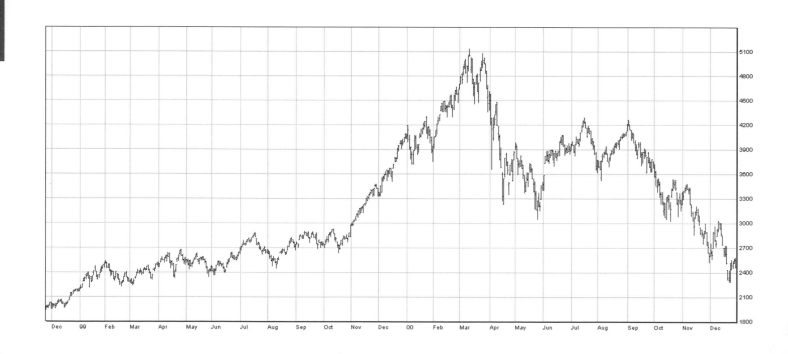

Bubbles like this have been around since tulip mania gripped Holland in the 1630s (individual bulbs sold for the equivalent of $10,000 today).

Bubbles even appear in computer simulations of the stock market.

And they will doubtless appear in the real market again.

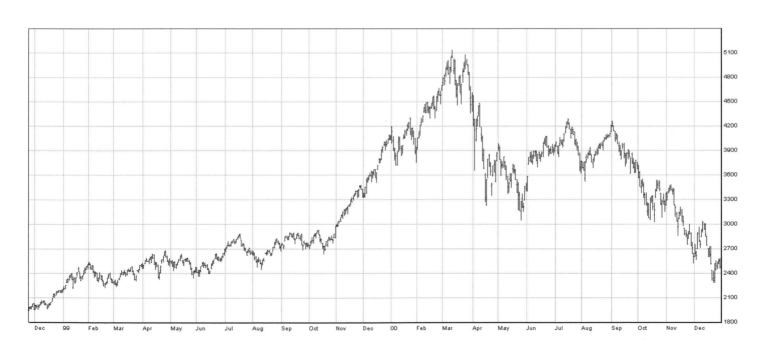

So, if you beat the market: congratulations!

You can safely say you know your way around a stock chart.

Remember to practice on other charts within a week, else your skills will fade.

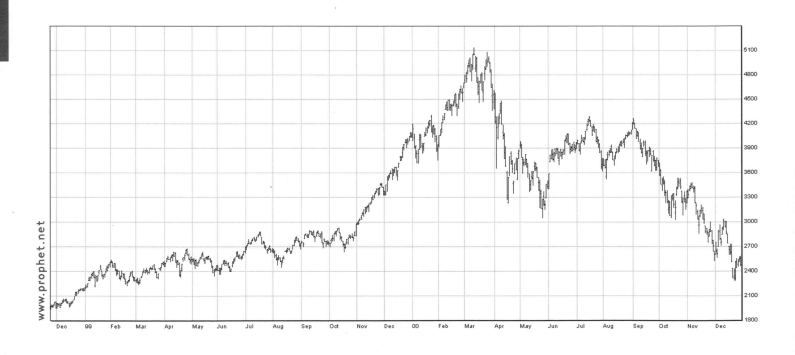

Pause point

Take a break after reading this page.

As before, you'll get most from this book if you stop here and return a few days later. If possible, get some practice with real charts in the meantime. There are two copies (so you can pull one out) of a pattern map you may find helpful starting after page 234.

The next section, the Epilogue, recaps everything you have learned so far. It doesn't introduce any new patterns; instead, it helps you hone your skills.

You know enough by now to find the Next Steps section interesting. It starts on page 229 and has pointers to a variety of resources you can use to build on the hooks you have installed in your head so far.

Epilogue

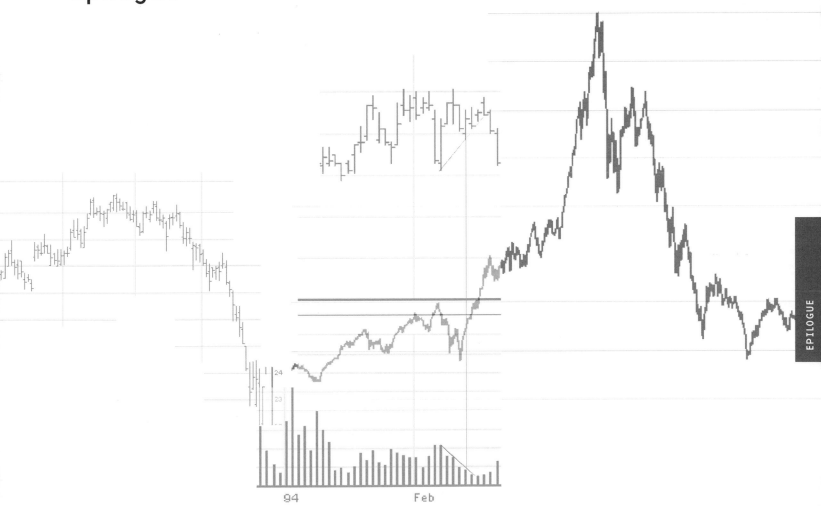

Let's review trends and patterns before turning to an intriguing chart.

The stock below is Pixar, the computer animation company responsible for *Toy Story* and *A Bug's Life*.

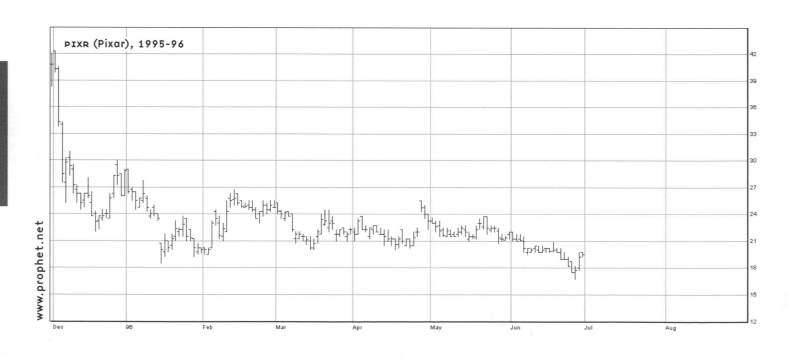

PIXR (Pixar), 1995-96

www.prophet.net

Pixar went public shortly after the enormous success of *Toy Story* in late 1995, which is where this chart starts.

Draw the recent trendlines on this chart and forecast the next move. (Recall that trendlines can cut a bar or two so long as they have three good touches.)

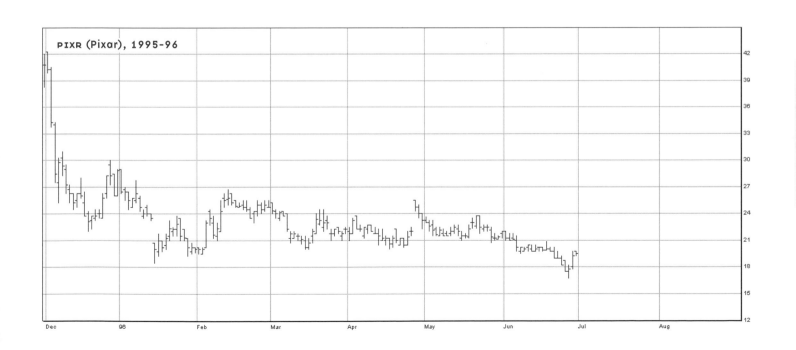

PIXR (Pixar), 1995-96

EPILOGUE

Over-hyping a new stock can do long term damage, as either of these trendlines would tell you.

Pixar lost 70% of its value in the nine months following its debut on the stock market.

PIXR (Pixar), 1995-96

Previous page

Dec   96   Feb   Mar   Apr   May   Jun   Jul   Aug

Remember Nokia's meteoric rise? It formed a classic pattern towards the end of its run.

Draw the recent trendlines, then see if you can name the pattern and the next move it suggests for this chart.

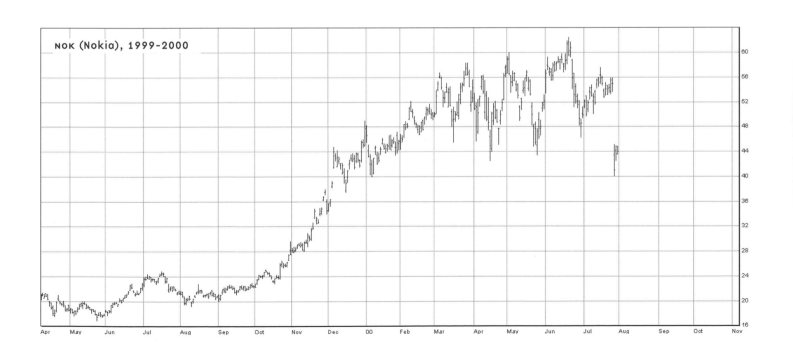

NOK (Nokia), 1999-2000

A megaphone—a bearish
pattern, suggesting a
downward move.

NOK (Nokia), 1999-2000

Previous
page

There is a long lower trendline
and a short upper trendline at
the rightmost end of this chart.
Go ahead and draw them both.

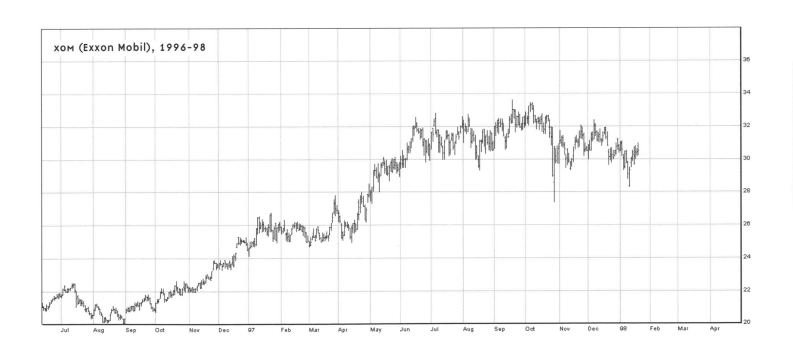

XOM (Exxon Mobil), 1996-98

An uptrend ending with a
symmetrical triangle. It is
difficult to predict which way a
chart will come out of a
symmetrical triangle until you
get a breakout…

XOM (Exxon Mobil), 1996-98

Here is the breakout. Would you buy, sell, or hold XOM now?

XOM (Exxon Mobil), 1996-98

Previous page

Buy.

XOM (Exxon Mobil), 1996-98

Previous page

And in this chart there are no less than five patterns: two symmetrical triangles, a megaphone, an ascending triangle, and a descending triangle.

Try finding at least two of them.

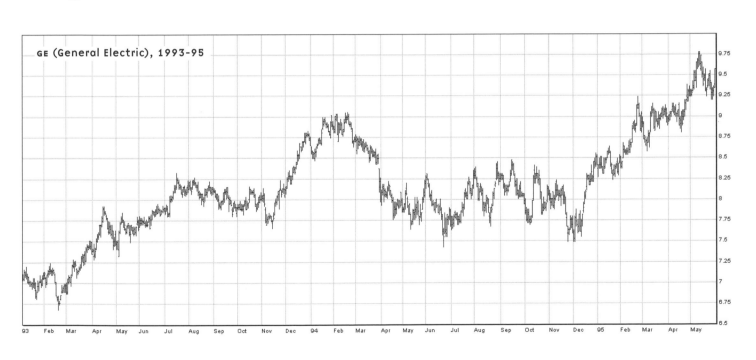

GE (General Electric), 1993-95

Not all charts are this busy of course.

If you found other patterns, check that your trendlines have enough touch points.

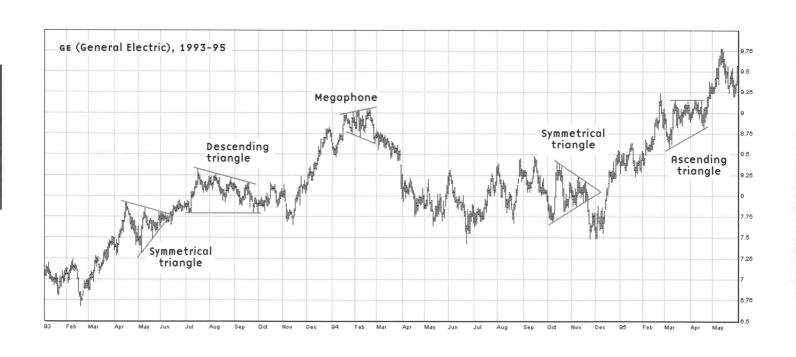

GE (General Electric), 1993-95

Megaphone

Descending triangle

Symmetrical triangle

Symmetrical triangle

Ascending triangle

Symmetrical triangle

Another chart. What pattern has just formed in it and what move does it suggest?

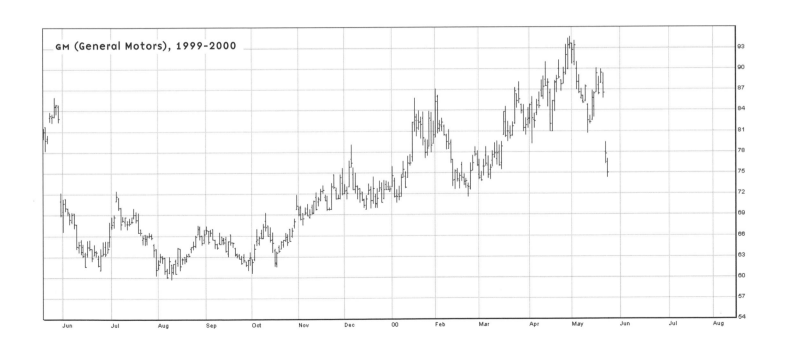

GM (General Motors), 1999–2000

A head and shoulders top
—bearish.

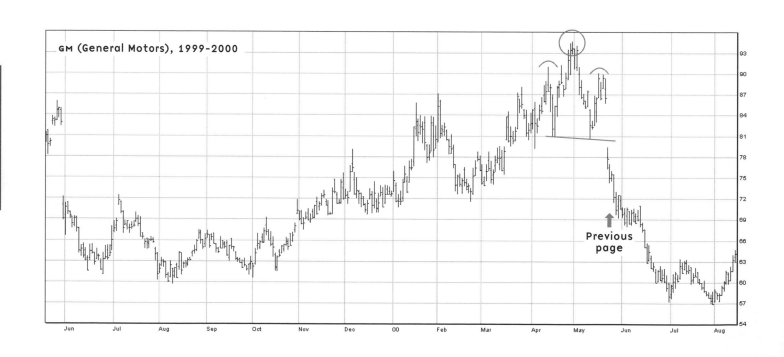

GM (General Motors), 1999-2000

Previous page

Draw the most recent support
line on this chart.

What would you do here? Buy,
sell, or hold?

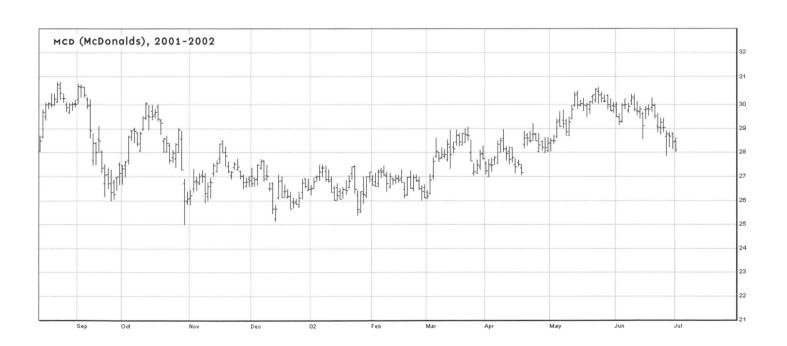

MCD (McDonalds), 2001-2002

The 'rules' say the most likely outcome is a bounce. But this stock fell right through support.

If you owned $100,000 of McDonalds, you lost $12,000 in a month.

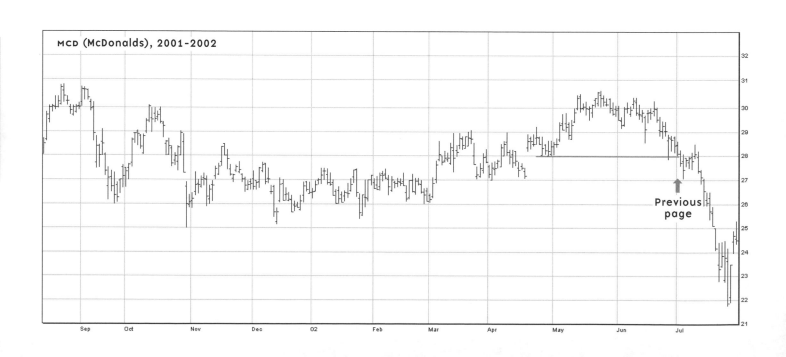

MCD (McDonalds), 2001-2002

Previous page

The rules don't work every time. The trick is to minimize your losses when they don't.

What could you have done to minimize your losses here? (Hint: it's the most important concept in this book.)

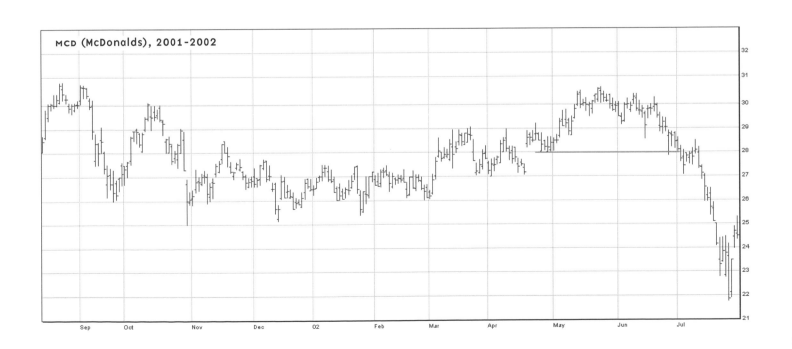

MCD (McDonalds), 2001-2002

Set a stop loss.

Set it at a level where, if the investment goes bad, you lose only what you can afford to lose.

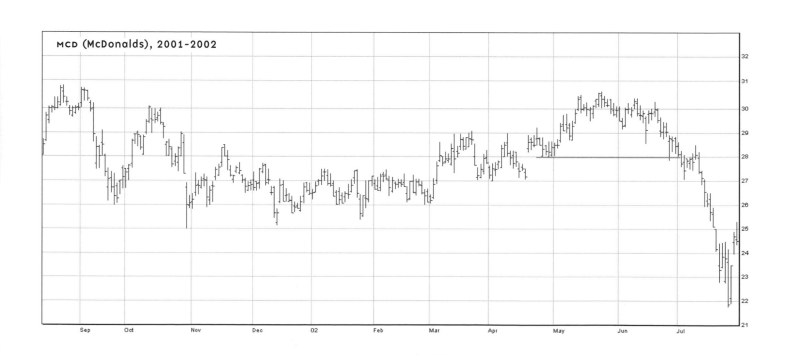

MCD (McDonalds), 2001-2002

You may not be familiar with this stock, but it will tell you a fascinating story.

The Mexico Fund invests in Mexican companies. This is late 1993, with the US locked in a closely fought debate over NAFTA.

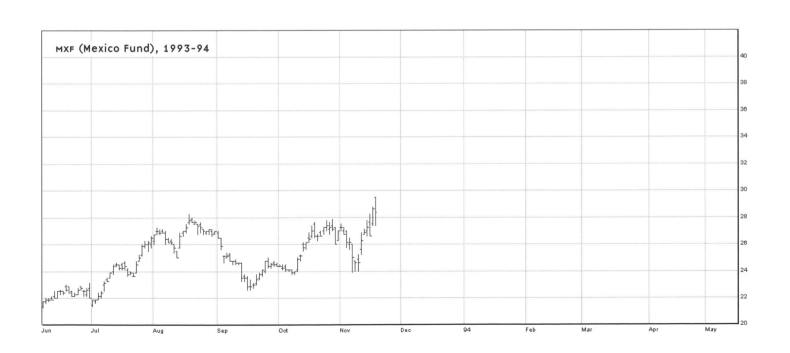

MXF (Mexico Fund), 1993-94

In mid-November, after weeks of suspense and bargaining, the House of Representatives passed NAFTA 234 votes to 200.

MXF quickly developed an up-sloping channel. In six weeks, it climbed from $28 to $39 on December 31. NAFTA came into effect the next morning.

MXF (Mexico Fund), 1993-94

Previous
page

EPILOGUE

That day, New Years Day 1994, a group of Mexicans called the Zapatistas staged a rebellion. The stock began a new phase.

So, draw the new upper and lower trendlines and name the pattern you have drawn before flipping the page.

MXF (Mexico Fund), 1993-94

Previous page

A symmetrical triangle.

No easy way to forecast what will happen next until we get a breakout, although…

MXF (Mexico Fund), 1993-94

...the volume chart sometimes contains a clue. Which side do you think will win this tug of war?

(Hint: when volume falls—like it does here near the end of January and again mid-February—it means the short-term trend in the price chart at those points is weak.)

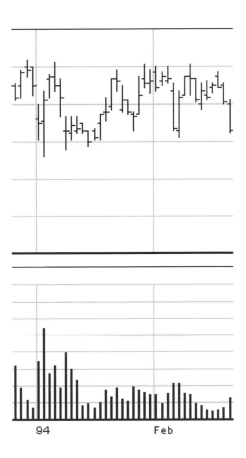

If volume falls when the chart climbs, it suggests buyers are not strong. The pattern could break to the downside.

Notice also the very low volume at the right. Low volume often comes before a big move, like a battle that appears finely balanced until one army begins to disintegrate and the battle is over very quickly.

And here is the breakout.

So now, what is your forecast for
this chart?

MXF (Mexico Fund), 1993-94

A significant decline: the losers accept defeat. With hindsight, $40 was too high for MXF. Too many people got on this bandwagon and it gave way.

Of course, those who were first on and first off the bandwagon did well. (Perhaps they read the chart.)

MXF (Mexico Fund), 1993-94

Previous page

Jun Jul Aug Sep Oct Nov Dec 94 Feb Mar Apr May

But what is most fascinating here is that the dramas in the stock chart (a steep climb; a sharp fall) unfolded weeks after the dramas in the world (NAFTA, Zapatistas).

In both cases, the real world event was followed by a signal in the chart and then a major move. And in both cases, it took time for the move to play itself out.

MXF (Mexico Fund), 1993-94

Clearly, it helps to be able to
read both chart events and
world events.

You are now one of the few
people equipped to do both.

MXF (Mexico Fund), 1993-94

www.prophet.net

If you have read each page up to this one, you will never look at a stock chart the same way again.

NASDAQ Composite Index, bubble of 2000

There is, of course, much more to it than we had the space to cover.

But you have the beginnings of a map in your head on which to build.

Dow Jones Industrial Average, crash of 1987

And you have a window into the workings of the financial world and the minds of those who have made or lost fortunes in it.

Dow Jones Industrial Average, crash of 1929

Thank you.

Tulip mania, Holland, 1630s

Next Steps

Now that you know your way around a stock chart, there is much more you can explore. We've included enough here to keep you busy and there is more at www.stikky.com/stockcharts, which is updated frequently.

Where to find charts

Several **websites** provide powerful charting for free. They use delayed data, meaning they include all but the last 20 minutes of prices—plenty good enough for finding medium-term trends and patterns. Some of the best are:

- www.prophet.net, a comprehensive browser-based site, used to produce the charts in this book
- www.bigcharts.com (part of *CBS MarketWatch*)
- www.stockcharts.com
- www.clearstation.com (a subsidiary of *E*Trade*).

When you open an account with a discount broker (see below), you will get access to their charting software and, usually, real-time rather than delayed prices.

SignalWatch, at www.signalwatch.com, is one of the few places you can find charts with suggested trendlines attached, so you can compare them with your own. You will also find charts in the financial press—the *Wall Street Journal*, *Financial Times*, etc—but rarely a technical analysis of them since this is still considered too whiskery by traditional media. And, since charts make poor TV (and worse radio), they seldom get more than a few seconds air time.

Chart software packages

Pre-internet, a dedicated package was the only way to generate charts (which explains the dramatic rise in charting since the arrival of the internet). These packages have evolved into powerful tools. For instance, some will let you draw a trendline and be alerted (at your cellphone perhaps) whenever the chart crosses the line.

- *AmiBroker*, www.amibroker.com
- *eSignal*, www.esignal.com
- *MetaStock* and *MetaStock Pro*, www.metastock.com
- *OmniTrader*, www.nirvanasystems.com, draws trendlines for you
- *Pristine ESP*, www.pristine.com
- *QCharts*, http://finance.lycos.com
- *Realtick*, www.realtick.com
- *TC2000*, www.wordenbrothers.com
- *TradeStation*, www.tradestation.com, expensive but awesome.

There are also extensions to many of these packages: www.equis.com sell add-ons that identify trends and patterns, and those at www.sr-analyst.com can find support and resistance lines automatically.

More patterns

You already know the major chart patterns. After those, the most widely followed are:

- *Head and shoulders bottom* and *double bottom*, which are the same as the top patterns you know, only the other way up
- *Triple top* and *triple bottom*, three peaks (or troughs) instead of two, so rarer than double tops and bottoms
- *Gaps*, whenever today's bar does not overlap with yesterday's
- *Dead cat bounce*, the colorful name for a chart that drops, then bounces up a little, usually meaning it will drop again
- *Rounding top* and *rounding bottom*, when the chart forms a dome or saucer shape
- *Wedge*, formed by two upward-sloping or downward-sloping lines that are not parallel (a sort of messy *channel*)
- *Flags* and *pennants*, which are mini versions of the *channel* and *wedge* respectively, pointing in the opposite direction to the trend and usually meaning that the trend will continue after the market has taken a breather.

Few analysts follow more patterns than that, though *The Encyclopedia of Chart Patterns* by Thomas N Bulkowski lists no fewer than 47. It also gives their frequency of occurrence and 'failure rate' (though it's not clear how this is calculated).

There are dozens of other **books** on interpreting stock charts—search any online bookstore for 'stock charts', 'technical analysis', or 'stock trading'. The authority on trendlines and patterns is *Technical Analysis of Stock Trends* by Robert D Edwards, John Magee, and Charles Bassetti, first published in 1948 and now in its eighth edition. It's not without faults (including the price) but it's definitive: when analysts disagree, this is the book they turn to.

Infuriatingly, most of these books differ from each other (and from the one you're holding) on issues as basic as what makes a good trendline—for instance requiring only two touches instead of three, which makes just about everything a trend.

Chart indicators

Looking out the window of a moving car, can you tell what speed it's going? All the information you need is there, but it can be difficult to gauge, which is why you have a speedometer. Similarly, there are speedometers for charts—known as 'indicators'—to help you track chart characteristics that are otherwise difficult to gauge. Here we look at three of the most popular: moving averages, RSI, and MACD. Most of the chart sources listed above can display these indicators and more.

The *moving average* draws a smooth line through a bumpy chart by averaging prices across several bars. Often the underlying trend is revealed. The 200-day moving average, which is the most widely used, reveals the long-term trend. The moving average behaves like the medium-term trendlines you have been drawing (but curvy instead of straight): when the chart approaches a moving average line, the most likely outcome is for it to bounce off. If it breaks through, it will most likely carry on in the same direction.

The chart indicator most similar to a speedometer is the *Relative Strength Indicator* (RSI). The most commonly used RSI, the 14-day RSI, moves in a range from 0 to 100. A high RSI means the chart is racing higher, possibly too quickly if RSI gets above 70. So, if RSI is above 70 and then crosses back below 70, that's seen as a good time to sell since things have gotten overheated. Similarly, a low RSI means the market is racing lower, possibly too quickly if RSI gets below 30. So an RSI that has been below 30 and then climbs above is taken as a signal to buy. A mid-range RSI (holding in the 30 to 70 range) indicates a balanced market.

The other widely used indicator is MACD ("mac-dee"). When you plot MACD on a chart you will see two lines: one that zips around (the 'fast' line) and another that is more measured and smoother (the 'slow' line). When the fast line crosses above the slow line, that's a buy signal; when it crosses below the slow line, that's a sell signal. It's as if the fast line leads the way.

If these three aren't enough for you, try also *Money Flow*, which combines volume and price in one indicator, and *Bollinger Bands*.

Advanced technical analysts even draw trendlines on the indicator charts and discern patterns, such as double tops, in them! When the main chart shows one trend, say up, and the indicator shows the opposite trend, the expectation is that the main chart will change direction. The indicator leads the way.

Online charting sites have more detailed descriptions of how to read these indicators and one of the better books on the subject is *Essential Technical Analysis* by Leigh Stevens.

Choosing a broker

Brokers come in four varieties: full-service, discount, super-discount, and active trader brokers.

Full-service brokers are the most expensive and offer stock-picking advice and research. They include *Charles Schwab, Fidelity, Merrill Lynch, Morgan Stanley,* and *Salomon Smith Barney.*

Discount brokers don't provide personalized advice, but charge a fraction of the price of a full-service broker (most of whom offer a discount service too):

- *Ameritrade*, www.ameritrade.com
- *Charles Schwab*, www.schwab.com
- *E*Trade*, www.etrade.com
- *Fidelity*, www.fidelity.com
- *HARRISdirect*, www.harrisdirect.com
- *Scottrade*, www.scottrade.com
- *Siebert*, www.siebertnet.com, which targets female investors
- *TD Waterhouse*, www.tdwaterhouse.com.

Super-discount brokers, such as *BuyandHold* (www.buyandhold.com) and *ShareBuilder* (www.sharebuilder.com), charge very low commissions but only allow trades to be made at certain pre-determined times.

Brokers for active traders (a polite term for 'day traders') offer sophisticated software and order placement priced for people who trade every day. They include *CyberTrader* (part of Schwab), *Power E*Trade*, and *TradeStation.*

SmartMoney magazine (www.smartmoney.com/brokers) and *Gómez* (www.gomezadvisors.com) provide free rankings of brokers; *SmartMoney* includes a table comparing fees.

Eight steps to begin trading

1. Choose a **broker**, open an account, and put some cash in it. Most brokers will let you start small. You'll need to decide between a cash and a margin account (margin means you can trade with borrowed money) and whether to request a facility to trade in stock options as well as stocks (not for beginners).

2. Make some practice trades at an **online trading simulator** such as www.marketsim.com or www.virtualstockexchange.com to make sure you understand what's going on.

3. Consider getting **tax advice**. If you make a profit, you will have to pay tax on it. Depending on your situation, there may be ways to reduce the amount you have to pay.

4. Learn about **order types** so you can fine tune the orders you place: *market*, *limit*, and *stop*. A *market order*, as you know, means you trade at whatever price prevails at the time. If you want to pay $30 and that's your limit, you place a *limit order* (but if the price stays higher than $30, your order won't be filled). If you want to sell as soon as the price drops to $20 you place a *stop order* (like a stop loss). Your broker's site should explain in more detail.

5. Have a **crash plan** ready if (when) the market crashes since you may not be able to reach your broker online. For instance, make a note of your broker's phone number and your account number so you can get out of the market in a hurry if you decide to. Being locked in when prices are spiralling down is no fun.

6. Decide your **stop loss**: the dollar amount that, if you lose it on any single stock, will trigger you to close out the position automatically, without a thought, leaving you to lick your wounds and look forward to a better trade.

7. When you are ready, **trade**. Start with small amounts; there is usually no minimum order size. You may be surprised to learn that you can't trade 24 hours a day. The New York Stock Exchange and Nasdaq, for instance, open at 9:30am and close at 4pm Eastern. Your broker may be able to fill a trade a bit earlier and a bit later, though the price may be worse.

8. Learn about **short sales**. Most brokers will allow you to sell stock you don't own. Why would you want to do this? If you think a stock price is going to go down, you can sell it and buy it back later at a lower price. Most beginning investors avoid selling short, but they are missing potential profits.

Sources of stock information

The main source of information for chartists is, of course, the chart. But charts reflect sentiment, so sounding out sentiment can help confirm (or otherwise) your reading of a chart.

To best gauge **sentiment**, read several different opinions. This is not difficult, since there are hundreds of sources. Some good starting points are: www.briefing.com, www.cnnfn.com, www.fool.com, www.investors.com, www.marketwatch.com, www.schaeffersresearch.com (which has a 'sentiment brief'), www.sentimentrader.com (subscription only), www.thestreet.com, the widely reported *Investor's Intelligence* weekly sentiment survey, and the financial press: *Wall Street Journal*, *New York Times*, *Financial Times*, *Economist*, *Barron's*, *BusinessWeek* and cable channels such as *Bloomberg TV*. (Some people would add message boards such as http://finance.yahoo.com to this list, but beware: these seldom contain balanced or well-informed comments.)

A widely held view, known as 'contrary opinion', is that when sentiment is excessively optimistic, markets are likely to fall (and *vice versa*). Historically, though, there has been a delay before the market turns—often several months.

Another category of stock information is **fundamental analysis**: earnings reports, company announcements, official filings, analysis of financials, etc. These will be covered at many of the same places listed above plus *Zacks* (www.zacks.com), *Hoovers* (www.hoovers.com) and the SEC's EDGAR (www.sec.gov/edgar.shtml and www.freeedgar.com) for official company filings. In theory, chartists can ignore fundamentals since they all feed into sentiment and the chart.

Other types of investments

Anything you can buy and sell in a financial market is called a **security**. This book has focused exclusively on stock charts since stocks are the most widely held securities by far. But all securities have price charts with trends and patterns.

A **stock** is a share in a company. Owning a stock means you own part of the company, though usually too small a part to have much say (Microsoft has issued ten billion shares, enough for everyone). Still, most shares come with the right to vote at shareholder meetings and the right to dividends paid by the company. Companies sell shares in themselves as a cheap way to raise money. It's cheap because there is a risk: shareholders are last in line for what's left if the company goes bust. (Think a big

company could never go bust? So did the shareholders of Enron.) The first time a company offers its stock for sale to the public is called an Initial Public Offering or IPO.

When you buy a **bond**, you are loaning the company money instead of buying part of it. You get paid interest each year and you get the original cost of the bond back when it expires. Bonds are less risky than shares since bondholders get paid before shareholders in the event the company goes bust. You can also buy government bond, known as Treasuries. Since the US government is not expected to go bust (it can always raise taxes), government bonds are considered the least risky of all.

A **mutual fund** is a basket of stocks and bonds chosen for you by a fund manager. The fund manager charges for his efforts, which are not necessarily any better than the market index.

A special, and relatively new, type of stock that tracks a market index is the **Exchange Traded Fund**. An ETF lets you buy a share in an index like the Dow Jones Industrial Average (DJIA). They are simple, free of overheads (unlike mutual funds) and hugely popular. The major ETFs are:

- DIA, or 'diamonds', tracks the DJIA index
- QQQ, known as 'triple Q' or 'cubes', tracks the NASDAQ 100 (which is similar to the widely quoted NASDAQ Composite)
- SPY, known as 'spiders', tracks the Standard & Poor's 500.

Commodities are physical things such as gold, oil, coffee, or pork bellies. Since you probably don't want to take delivery of large quantities of these goods, you would typically use a special security called a **futures contract** to invest in them. This is an agreement to buy the commodity in the future; you buy and sell the futures contract rather than the commodity itself.

Foreign exchange means currencies: the dollar, the yen, the euro, the British pound, etc. It's usually abbreviated to 'forex' since no-one on Wall Street has the time to say "foreign exchange".

Options give you the right to buy (or sell) another security in the future. (Unlike a futures contract, you don't *have* to buy the underlying security—you have the option.) They are more complex and higher risk than stocks but potentially higher return.

There's a financial dictionary at www.investopedia.com.

Expos, education, magazine(s)

There are no **expos** focusing exclusively on technical analysis, though you'll find enclaves at these major investment shows (both now run by the same company): *The Money Show* (www.intershow.com) and *The International Traders Expo* (www.tradersexpo.com).

The *Market Technicians Association* (www.mta.org) and the *International Federation of Technical Analysts* (www.ifta.org) offer **qualifications** in technical analysis.

Technical Analysis of Stocks & Commodities **magazine** is dedicated to technical analysis; subscribe at www.traders.com. Most of its content is oriented towards full-time day traders but some is for less experienced readers. A bonus issue published every January reports the best brokers, software, courses, and websites according to a reader poll (some of the same information is on the Traders' Resource section of the website).

Advanced stuff

- *Cycle theory* software, such as www.mesasoftware.com, finds the recurring cycles in a chart

- *Filter* software, such as www.jurikres.com, smooths price charts mathematically to reveal the underlying trend

- *Genetic algorithms*, such as www.tradingsolutions.com, 'evolve' trading systems

- *Neural nets*, such as www.neuroshell.com, find patterns that humans have a tough time seeing

- *Programmable* systems, such as www.wealth-lab.com and www.tradestation.com, let you build and test your own trading system.

Things to avoid (in our opinion)

- Alternative charts: candlesticks and point-and-figure charts have their fans but neither offers anything over the OHLC charts you used in this book. (Log scale charts, on the other hand, are worth using for very long-range analysis).

- Mechanical trading systems: tell you when to buy and sell but don't reveal why. They claim incredible returns over the last X years, provided X is carefully chosen so as to demonstrate their success.

- Unsubstantiated theories: Wave Theory, Fibonacci price targets.

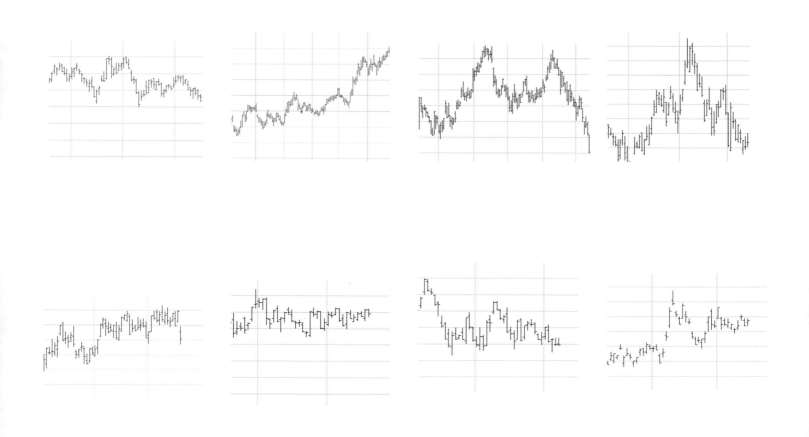

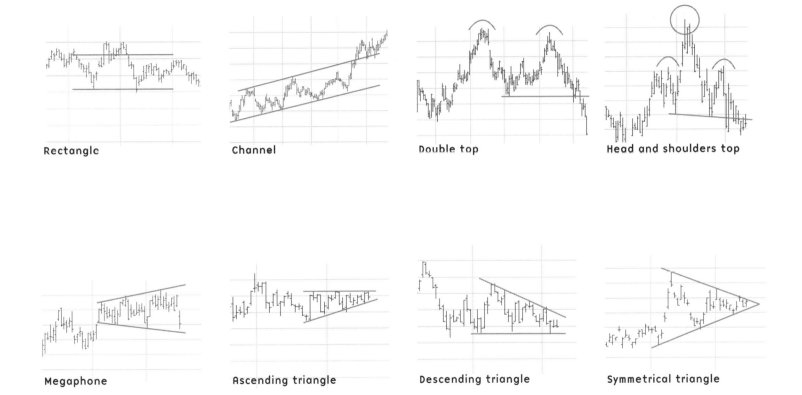

Rectangle

Channel

Double top

Head and shoulders top

Megaphone

Ascending triangle

Descending triangle

Symmetrical triangle

Stock chart pattern map from the book *Stikky Stock Charts*. www.stikky.com

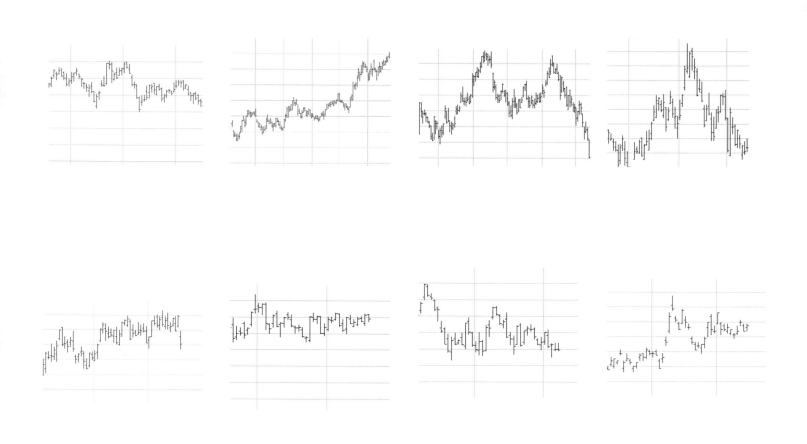

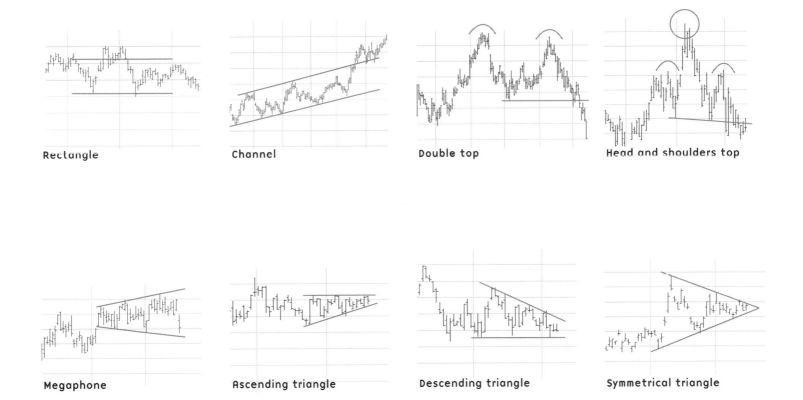

Rectangle

Channel

Double top

Head and shoulders top

Megaphone

Ascending triangle

Descending triangle

Symmetrical triangle

Stock chart pattern map from the book *Stikky Stock Charts*. www.stikky.com

About Stikky books

The Stikky story

We started publishing Stikky books in 2003 after a web-based trial generated far more interest than we expected. Our first book, *Stikky Night Skies*, took a year to create.

The series covers topics we believe will be of value and interest to anyone. We created it because we couldn't find a 'how to' book that took into account recent findings about how people learn. Instead, they often provide too much information and structure it in a way that makes sense to experts but not to beginners. According to our research, most people read less than half of 'how to' books they buy.

The Stikky approach

- Start with small pieces of knowledge and systematically build them into a comprehensive picture
- Make the practice environment as similar as possible to the real world
- Organize the topic around readers' goals such as: How do I minimize losses?
- Provide plenty of practice—80% of learning is really re-learning so we stage multiple opportunities to test and reinforce your knowledge
- Make it fun.

How we create a Stikky book

Each book is prepared with the help of subject experts, some of whom are named on the cover. It goes through multiple rounds of review by Test Readers. (If you would like to become a Stikky Test Reader, visit www.stikky.com). We record every time they get stuck, together with hundreds of other suggestions, and make careful changes. Then we go through the whole process again.

Everything about the product in your hands was informed by this research: the format, the binding, even the name. And we only publish a book when we know it works.

Our charity pledge

We promise to spend 10% of profits from the series on knowledge-based charity. We believe that knowledge generates independence and so is a liberating form of aid.

Upcoming Stikky books

Future titles may cover topics such as the secrets of persuasion or improving your memory. If there are topics you would like to see included in the series, suggest them at www.stikky.com, where you will also find news of additions to the series before their publication.

What our readers say

Comments from readers of Stikky books

15 minutes with this book was more valuable than the 3 hours I spent stumbling with another. *BM, USA*

Amazing…so simple and so thorough. *MW, UK*

After running through the sequence, I was able to locate all the points very quickly, can't wait to try it out. *PP, Australia*

Within 30 minutes this book has provided a basis for me to begin a new adventure and hobby. *BR, Indiana*

Yes, my brain is full, and I don't have time to learn anything new. But the folks who created this book are on to something. *A reader from Palo Alto, California*

If you've ever had a teacher who explained things in such a way that they stikk to your mind forever, this book will let you re-live that experience. *SN, New Jersey*

I felt successful from the start. *JC, UK*

This book at first seemed too simple. Then after buying and reading it, I realized it was perfect. The information is presented in such a way that I feel I'll retain the knowledge for life. *A reader from Dallas, Texas*

I have read many, many books on constellations, but this is the most effective one I have ever seen. *WR, Canada*

Now I can observe and understand with confidence. Thank you so much. *LC, Michigan*

Thank you so much for making things so easy. I feel like I've made a start, at long last. *CW, England*

We need more teachers/educators with this approach. *JF, USA*

What a magnificent idea! I will email everybody I know that even MIGHT be interested! Please PLEASE create more of these. *DJ, Ohio*

Beautifully simple, entertaining and delightful. *PL, Ontario*

Thank You

Quentin Ball · Jonathan Bloom · Victoria Cable-Kulli · Simon Chiang · Helen Crawley · Merry Davis
Tristan George · Chi Huang · Andrew Lyons · Miranda McGrath · Alix Martin · Nell Montgomery
Clive Murray · John Oakes · Earle Sandberg · Leah Soufrant · Clare Smith · Amy Wong · Nadia Zia